AF470702

# BUSES IN CAMERA:
## South-East

DJG 610C
EAST KENT
LONDON

# BUSES IN CAMERA:
# South-East

**John Parke**



LONDON
**IAN ALLAN LTD**

First published 1981

ISBN 0 7110 0878 7





Published by Ian Allan Ltd, Shepperton, Surrey; and printed by Ian Allan Printing Ltd at their works at Coombelands in Runnymede, England

Title page: *This 1972 view of Victoria Coach Station typifies a Saturday of the period with East Kent AEC Reliances on the departure platforms and Maidstone & District AEC Reliances and Leyland Leopards setting down. Traffic on coastal services from London has decreased greatly in recent years.*

# Contents



## Photo credits

J. M. Aldridge: 79 (bottom), 80 (top); Ian Allan Library: 11 (bottom), 17 (bottom), 51, 62 (bottom); D. Barrow: 27 (top); Michael Bennett: 31 (bottom); Gavin Booth: 28 (top); S. J. Brown: 22 (bottom), 26 (top); W. T. Cansick: 39 (bottom), 40 (top), 44 (bottom), 46 (bottom), 50 (bottom), 57 (top), 112 (bottom); J. G. Carroll: 59 (centre); E. C. Churchill: 70 (top); R. N. Collins: 58 (bottom); T. Coughlin: 17 (centre), 39 (centre); B. C. Coward: 56 (bottom); John Crittenden: 67 (top), 72 (bottom); Richard Delahoy: 16 (top), 37 (bottom), 48 (bottom); K. Dent: 39 (top); T. H. J. Detheridge: 31 (top); M. Dryhurst: 11 (top), 12, 37 (centre), 48 (top), 53 (bottom), 55 (top), 59 (top), 66 (bottom), 69 (bottom), 71 (top), 77 (bottom), 78 (top), 86 (centre), 93 (bottom); R. A. Flower: 100; M. Fowler: 94 (top); A. R. J. Frost: 23 (bottom), 50 (top), 101 (top); P. R. Gainsbury: 66 (top), 68; P. J. Gilbert: 58 (top); G. K. Gillberry: 34 (bottom), 82 (bottom), 84 (top), 93 (top), 98 (top); D. Fereday Glenn: 60 (top), 61 (top); Mr & Mrs P. Haines: 40 (bottom); Hants & Dorset: 60 (bottom); W. J. Haynes: 38 (top); JD Transport Photographs: 19 (top); B. L. Jackson: 26 (bottom), 28 (bottom), 64 (bottom), 65 (top); H. N. James: 17 (top); B. A. Jenkins: 10 (bottom); Kevin Lane: 15 (top); B. S. Lewendon: 19 (bottom), 27 (bottom), 33 (bottom), 82 (top); J. G. Lidstone: 16 (bottom), 38 (bottom); M & D and East Kent Bus Club: 29 (top), 55 (bottom), 64 (top), 83, 86 (bottom); A. R. Macfarlane: 56 (top); J. L. Manley: 36 (bottom), 101 (bottom); J. Marsh: 110 (top); G. Mead: 79 (top), 80 (bottom); G. R. Mills: 14 (top), 15 (bottom), 20, 21 (top), 22, 23 (top), 24 (centre), 25 (top), 41, 42, 43 (top), 43 (bottom), 44 (top), 46 (top), 47, 48 (centre), 49 (bottom), 72 (top), 87 (top), 94 (bottom), 96 (bottom), 97 (top), 98 (centre), 99, 102, 103, 104, 105 (bottom), 106 (top), 107, 108, 109, 111 (top), 112 (top); G. R. Mortimer: 24 (bottom), 105 (bottom), 106 (bottom), 111 (bottom), 112 (bottom); T. W. Moore: 2, 73 (bottom), 74 (top), 76 (top); A. Moyes: 77 (top); J. R. Neale: 9 (top), 45, 95, 96 (top); P. R. Nuttall: 75, 81 (bottom), 92 (bottom); J. F. Parke: 7, 29 (centre), 29 (bottom), 52, 53 (top), 61 (centre), 62 (top), 63 (top), 73 (top), 76 (centre), 87 (bottom), 88, 89, 90; M. A. Penn: 13 (top), 30 (bottom), 33 (top), 81 (top), 110 (bottom); David Rendell: 30 (top); J. Rickard: 49 (top); Peter W. Robinson: 65 (bottom); T. E. Smith 55 (centre); B. W. Spencer: 18 (bottom), 54 (top), 86 (top); M. S. Stokes: 97 (bottom); D. M. Stuttard: 34 (top), 57 (bottom); Viewfinder: 8, 59 (bottom), 63 (centre), 63 (bottom), 67 (bottom), 70 (bottom), 71 (bottom), 76 (bottom), 84 (bottom), 91, 92 (top); Graham J. Wadley: 31 (centre), 36 (top), 85 (top); C. Wilkin: 69 (top); D. Withers: 74 (bottom); L. J. Wright: 14 (bottom), 50 (bottom); F. W. York: 5.

# Preface

This book presents, mainly pictorially, aspects of public service vehicle operation over the past 40 years in the South Eastern and Eastern traffic areas and so ends the initial treatment of the mainland of Britain in this *Buses in Camera* series. In common with other editors one has not found it easy to provide complete coverage of the many aspects of potential interest within the space available but the situation has been eased a little by the fact that earlier volumes have treated some operators which overlap into the area which one has sought to cover so that these have called for less attention. Furthermore John Gray's series on the London area has made it largely unnecessary to deal with the Metropolitan Traffic Area.

It has seemed easiest to divide the book into sections covering local authority operations, subsidiaries of the National Bus Company, South Eastern independents and, finally, their rather more numerous counterparts in East Anglia. In the endeavour to illustrate both wellknown and less usual types it has been possible in some cases to kill some birds with one stone with more than one vehicle in a picture. In other cases the practice of some independents of buying the secondhand buses of large operators has made it practicable to depict a widely-used type in a later guise.

Wherever possible the illustrations used have not previously been published and I must thank the many providers of them. Acknowledgements to known sources appear on page 4.

*John Parke*

Below: *This Leyland-bodied Leyland Titan in the King Alfred fleet of R. Chisnell and Sons, Winchester, had been rebuilt above the waistline by Reading, of Portsmouth, by the time this picture was taken on Magdalen Hill in 1964.*

# The Scene and its Background

Most parts of Britain have their own characteristics and this is certainly true of South-Eastern England and East Anglia. There is, of course, their nearness to London and with electrification of the railways there has been a marked widening of the area in which many residents commute regularly to and from the capital. The building of motorways and other road improvements have also had an influence in this regard. Somewhat paradoxically the wartime dispersal of industry led to the appearance of works in many districts previously considered basically agricultural and this trend has endured so that industrial estates have sprung up at many places sometimes on the sites of wartime aerodromes. Towns which already possessed some industry such as Ashford (Kent) and Basingstoke have been subjected to substantial expansion schemes and new towns have been set up at Crawley and at Basildon.

Such developments and the changes in educational policy with the closing of many village schools have influenced the pattern of bus timetables with a requirement for more peak hour journeys and, since the late 1950s, a lessening of the demand for offpeak or shopping journeys. The days when Saturdays in particular and summer Sundays to some degree used to produce really heavy traffic demand are now a matter of fading memory and many of the garages of the larger operators have fewer buses out on service on Saturdays than on Mondays to Fridays, while Sunday requirements are infinitesimal. This change in circumstances probably hit the south-east first, although it has since spread more and more, due, it is argued, to the higher proportion of cars per head of population than in other parts of the country. This led also to the faster changeover to one-man operation both on operating grounds from the economic viewpoint and because of difficulties in staff recruitment. It seems that the south east tends always to be in the van when conditions change for it took some years before reluctance to take up bus work became equally apparent further north despite worsening unemployment.

With the early start to the decline in bus travel after the glorious postwar peak, fleet sizes tended to decrease fairly rapidly although the urgent search for omo buses and subsequently the bus grant provisions served to camouflage the effect by provoking abnormally large orders for new vehicles. Many wartime deliveries with utility bodywork were given new bodies as opportunity offered and it was perhaps coincidental that their second useful life should have been approaching its end just as the new rear-engined double-deckers were appearing on the scene in quantity. Underfloor-engined single-deckers were longer established but floor heights were and, indeed, still are a problem when it is a question of bus work with only the Bristol RE and more recently the Leyland National seeming to provide an answer in quantity. Changes in bus fleets are inevitably reflected in the pictures which serve also to remind us that during the period has come the disappearance of trolleybuses from Bournemouth, Brighton,

Hastings, Ipswich, Maidstone, Portsmouth, Reading and Southend. In some ways the most marked change has been at Maidstone where the trolleybus replacement by double-deck buses gave ground subsequently to a policy of single-deck operation which led to the hiring out of double-deckers to others and to the subsequent sale of what was quite a modern fleet. Hiring has in recent years become almost a commonplace as has the transfer of vehicles from one National Bus Company subsidary to another. In addition the coalition of the management of some NBC companies such as the merger of Aldershot & District with Thames Valley and Hants & Dorset with Wilts & Dorset, the absorption of the Westcliff undertaking by Eastern National and of Brighton, Hove & District by Southdown, and the provision of common management for East Kent and Maidstone & District have all had their effect.

In the local authority sphere the Lowestoft undertaking, which had become Waveney under the 1974 reconstruction of local government, was wound up while there has been a trend towards closer collaboration with the appropriate NBC company in instances such as Bournemouth, Portsmouth and Southend.

Below: *The postwar Dennis Falcon was a relatively rare bird, but all the BET-associated companies in the South East operated some. One of the 15 which went to East Kent is seen in the then new Canterbury bus station.*

# Local Authorities

There were 12 local authority undertakings in the South Eastern and Eastern traffic areas at the beginning of the period under review and there are now 11, the Waveney undertaking, better remembered as Lowestoft Corporation having ceased to operate in 1970. All had tramway origins with the exception of Eastbourne which commenced motorbus operation on 12 April 1903 and was thus a municipal pioneer in this field. The progress from trams to trolleybuses involved Bournemouth (from 1933), Brighton (1939 when it also commenced motorbus operation), Ipswich, which commenced conversion in 1923 and completed it three years later whereafter it remained trolleybus-only for years, Maidstone (1928), Portsmouth (1934), Reading (from 1936) and Southend (from 1925). Colchester had completed its conversion from trams to motorbuses in December, 1929, Great Yarmouth in December, 1933, Lowestoft in 1931 and Southampton in 1941.

Below: *Bournemouth Transport livery has been modified to one of yellow with a blue flash as exemplified by Leyland Atlantean 251 seen at Iford Bridge near Boscombe.*

Right: *Making a feature of its open-top services during suitable weather Bournemouth operates a number of convertible Daimler Fleetlines. Some of these were, however, sold to London Transport in 1978 and one is seen near Marble Arch in August of that year.*

Below: *On 20 April 1969 the Bournemouth trolleybuses were withdrawn and Sunbeam 278 which headed the final procession along Castle Lane to the Mallard Road depot is seen decorated for the occasion.*

BOURNEMOUTH PIER
VIA
LANSDOWNE
39
G
ALJ 986
FANCY GOODS
SENIOR SERVICE

NO
ENTRY
Central Station
Kings Road
KINGS ROAD

Top left: *A rarer type of trolleybus was open-top 202 an earlier Sunbeam which also appeared in the final procession.*

Far left; *In contrast with the London view an open top Daimler Fleetline with Weymann bodywork is seen at Bournemouth Pier in the summer of 1965.*

Above: *Brighton Corporation commenced motorbus operation in 1939 and included in the first batch of AEC Regents was No 67 seen here on the right in a June 1961 view which features AEC trolleybuses 23 and 4 in their last month of operation and Leyland Titan PD2 No 6, one of the batch which replaced the last trolleybuses.*

Left: *Competition to board one of the new AEC trolleybuses when services began in 1939 on the Lewes Road route to be followed shortly by the remainder.*

Above: *84, a 1947 AEC Regent III with Weymann bodywork stands at Brighton station beside Brighton, Hove & District 418 (ex-6418) a 1950 Bristol K5G with all-metal ECW bodywork.*

Left: *Brighton took delivery of more AEC Regent IIIs with Weymann bodies in 1950. They included 92, seen here at Preston*

Top right: *After buying forward-entrance Leyland Titans, Brighton turned to rear-engined double-deckers and Willowbrook-bodied Leyland Atlantean No 81 is seen at Old Steine in May, 1971.*

Right: *One of the afore-mentioned forward-entrance Titans at the Hollingbury Estate terminus.*

45
SOUTH WOODINGDEAN
BEAL

Hanningtons
BRIGHTON'S
STORE
53
FOR
SOFT
FURNISHINGS
OLD STEINE
Build the world you want with The Builder
PAY
AS YOU
ENTER
5012 CD

ESSEN COUNTY STANDARD
THE NEWSPAPER OF NORTH ESSEX
ST. BOTOLPH'S
6
SVW 451

H·A·EVANS
HAIRDRESSERS
READ THE LOCAL
EVENING STAR
BEST FOR COLCHESTER
Jolliffe's
GARAGE
Baughans
46
KEV 331

Left: *Added to the Colchester fleet in 1951 was No 6, an all-Crossley DD42/7, seen here at Prettygate terminus, The Commons waiting to leave for St Botolphs in 1966 some two years before its withdrawal.*

Bottom left: *Delivered in 1945 with Duple austerity body. Colchester 46, a Bristol K6A still looked smart 19 years later.*

Right: *Massey bodywork was fitted to Colchester 36 a Leyland Titan PD2 seen climbing North Station Road towards the town in 1974.*

Below: *One of 11 AEC Regent Vs with Massey bodywork operated by Colchester is seen leaving Egerton Green Road.*

29A
IMPROVE YOUR HOME! RING
IPSWICH 50184/5
DOUBLE GLAZING
REPLACEMENT WINDOWS
COLCHESTER
23
OWC 723M

CADMAN
BUILDING CONTRACTORS
COLCHESTER
60
NIRIMBA
SOUTHEND
LEYLAND
ATLANTEAN
JHK 500N
COMPULSORY
BUS STOP

Left: *Hired to Southend Transport for four months in 1978 was Colchester 23, an ECW-bodied Bristol RELL seen here in Southend central bus station.*

Bottom left: *Also hired by Southend but for one day, Derby Day (1976), so that it could release its open-toppers for that occasion, was Colchester Leyland Atlantean 60 seen at Eastwood about to make its last journey on 29 to Southend before being returned.*

Top right: *Colchester Leyland Leopard 101 in Colchester in June, 1979 when working on hire to East Anglian Express to Great Yarmouth and the holiday camps. With it is Grey-Green Leopard en route from Harwich to London.*

Centre right: *One of the AEC Reliances originally Salford Corporation and subsequently Selnec PTE in service at Colchester.*

Below: *In 1936 Eastbourne Corporation, which had long been a Leyland purchaser, created some surprise by ordering three AEC Regents with Strachans bodywork — it ordered three Leyland Titans at the same time. No 92 seen here was the middle one of the batch.*

*Left: Eastbourne was among the earlier seaside municipalities to indulge again in open-top bus operation and, after converting some early TDs and later Titans and Regents, it came round to this somewhat unusual conversion by East Lancs, the original bodybuilder of this 1967 Titan PD2.*

*Below: Leyland Titan PD2 No 80 dating from 1966 seen after repainting in the new livery adopted in 1970.*

*Right: Eastbourne has never been an extensive user of single-deckers and the appearance of this Seddon midibus in 1973 came as something rather out of the ordinary. It took over a minibus operation.*

*Bottom right: Seen slightly removed from its usual beat this Leyland Atlantean wearing an allover advertising scheme was carrying spectators of the Historic Commercial Vehicle Club's London-to-Brighton run in 1974.*

EASTBOURNE CORPORATION
94
SEDDON
MJK 94L

6 A
SEAFRONT SERVICE
TO FOOT
OF BEACHY HEAD
KHC 816K
By Road or Rail, by Air or Sea —
All Travel starts at P.S.T.!
PERSONAL SERVICE TRAVEL
29 Grove Road Eastbourne & Branches
'Service is our middle name!
HERE COMES
THE P.S.T. BUS

Left: *One of 10 Massey-bodied Leyland Titan PD1s for Great Yarmouth in 1947, No 56, which was withdrawn in 1963, passed to Mulleys Motorways, Ixworth.*

Below: *Among the few local authorities to use the Albion Nimbus was Great Yarmouth. This 1959 example with Willowbrook bodywork was withdrawn in 1965 and passed to Booth & Fisher, Halfway.*

Right: *Another less usual type so far as municipalities were concerned was the Daimler Roadliner. Great Yarmouth 24 is seen on service 10.*

Bottom right: *Again a less frequent type was the AEC Swift. Not unreasonably the Great Yarmouth order specified Eastern Coach Works bodies for the later ones when ECW bodywork had become commercially available again. Earlier ones had Willowbrook bodies, but 81 was ECW.*

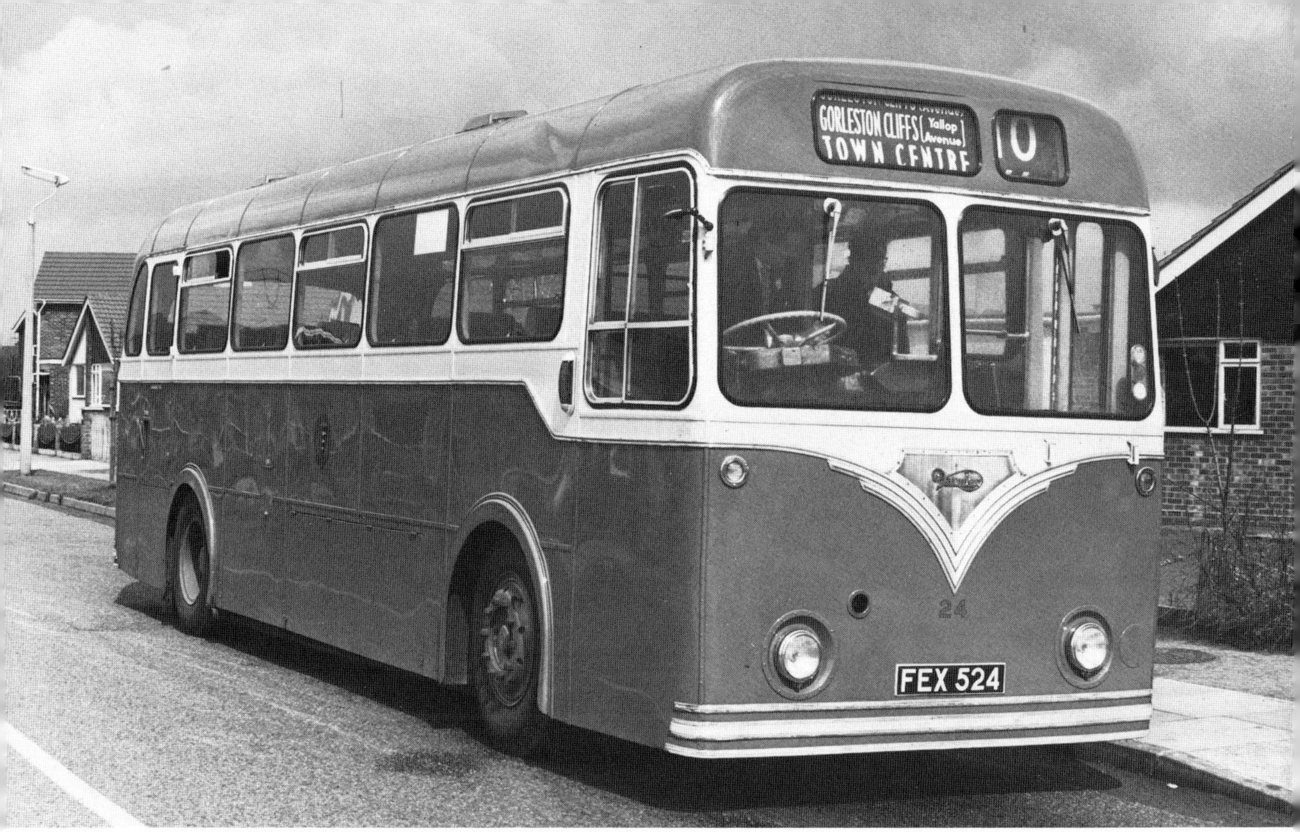

GORLESTON CLIFFS [ Yallop Avenue ]
TOWN CENTRE
24
FEX 524

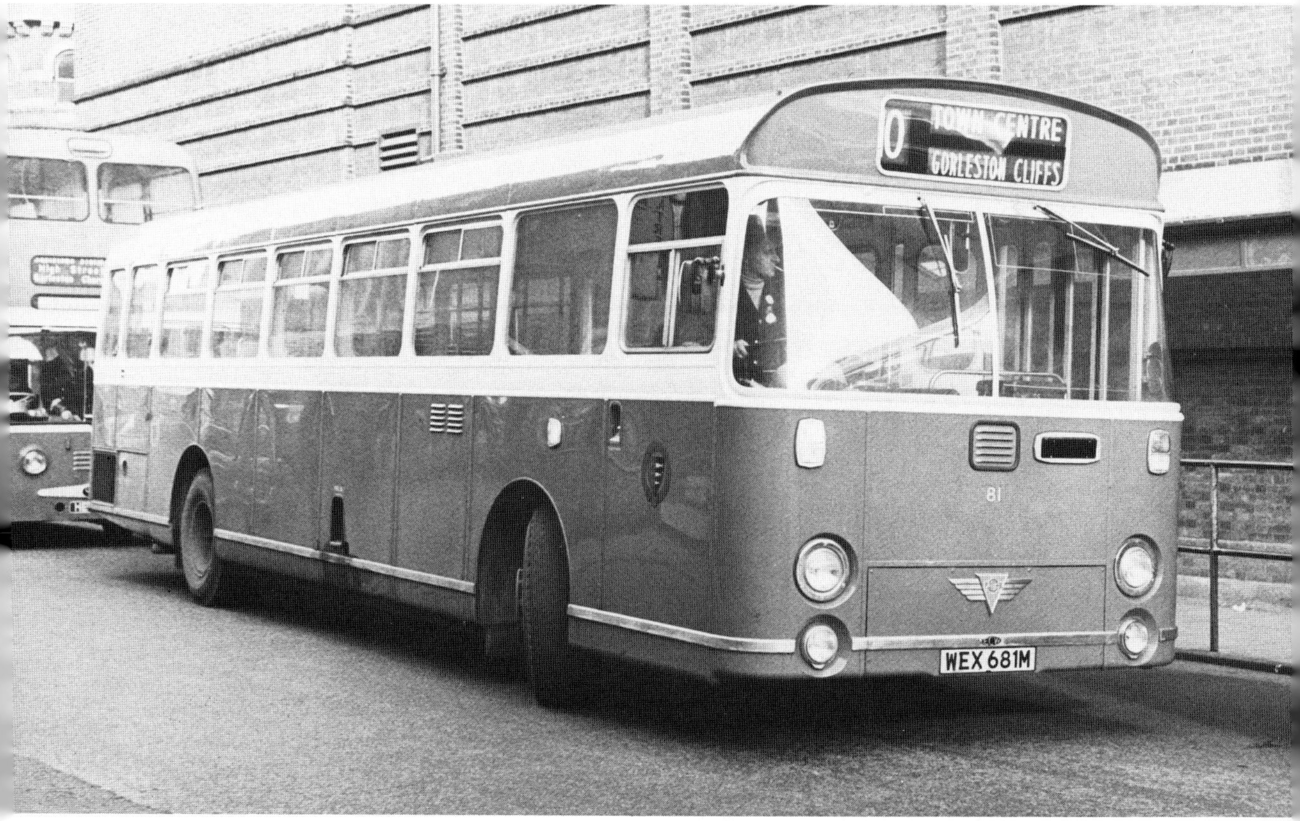

TOWN CENTRE
GORLESTON CLIFFS
81
WEX 681M

Left: *One of the Daimler Roadliners comes out to pass a forward-entrance Daimler CVG6 of Great Yarmouth.*

Centre left: *The earlier Atlanteans of Great Yarmouth are now being withdrawn. No 4 (DEX 704) is seen at North Denes.*

Below: *The first Bristols for Yarmouth were eight Gardner-engined Bristol VRTs with ECW bodies seating 77. No 34 is seen crossing the River Yare in May 1977.*

Above: *The first motorbuses operated by the Ipswich undertaking were six Park Royal-bodied AEC Regent IIIs of 1950. Nos 2 and 5 are seen at Electric House in 1968, their last year in service.*

Below: *A later AEC — No 25 a Regent V — still at work in East Anglia ferrying passengers and baggage between the Townsend Thoresen terminal and the ships plying between Felixstowe and Zeebrugge.*

Left: *Between 1926 and 1950 Ipswich solely operated trolleybuses and from 1933 to 1939 all were of local Ransomes, Sims and Jefferies manufacture. 86 was an odd-man out ordered in the summer of 1939.*

Centre left: *Passing Holywells Park at the junction of Nacton Road and Felixstowe Road this Sunbeam F4 with Park Royal body entered service in 1950 and was withdrawn when the trolleybuses were abandoned in 1963.*

Below: *With trolleybuses long departed this 1977 view at Electric House shows two of Ipswich Borough Transport's AEC Swifts and two Leyland Atlanteans.*

Right: *One of nine AEC Regent IIs with Eastern Coach Works bodies operated by Lowestoft in London Road North in May 1967. It was withdrawn six months later having entered service in 1947.*

Bottom right: *Leyland PD2A/30 with East Lancs body and No 9 in the fleet. It is passing Lowestoft Central Station in April 1965.*

TUTTLES
TUTTLES
Haig SCOTCH WHISKY in every Home
CRASKE
1 PAKEFIELD
20
GBJ 191

1 PAKEFIELD
LACONS BABY BROWN
LEYLAND
BRT 668C

Above: *In the 1969-73 period Lowestoft bought 10 ECW-bodied AEC Swifts. No 4 (YRT 898H), one of the first batch, is seen in Lowestoft in May 1977 carrying the Waveney fleetname some eight months before operations ceased.*

Left: *Maidstone Borough Transport has abandoned the use of double-deckers, but when No 75 seen here in 1966 was delivered in 1947 there was no such expectation nor of trolleybus abandonment. A Daimler CVG6 it had Northern Counties bodywork.*

Top right: *The trolleybus system was closed on 15 April 1967 but in this view taken the previous year at The Wheatsheaf Massey-bodied Leyland Atlantean 27 is working on the trolleybus service to Park Wood while Sunbeam trolleybus 65 prepares to fork right for Loose.*

Right: *Maidstone Corporation Leyland Titan PD2A/30 at Reading on hire to Alder Valley in May 1974. This was one of several examples of hiring to other undertakings.*

PARK WOOD
HKR 4

FOR KENT
READING
READ KM
NO ENTRY FOR BUSES
NO PARKING FOR PRIVATE CARS
ANTHONY ALLSOP ASSOCIATES LTP
SPECIALISTS IN COMMERCIAL E INDUSTRIAL INSURANCE + FREE ADVISORY SERVICE +
102 KING STREET, MAIDSTONE. TEL. 63825/61048
LEYLAND
516 RKR

WATERLOO STREET GARAGE
FOR KENT
BLUE DOOR
READ KM
AKE 148K

ROYAL INSURANCE
The Maidstone Borough Council
Lilac Leopard
SENACRE WOOD
HNU 120N

Top left: *In November 1971, this then new Leyland Atlantean with Northern Counties body (48:AKE 148K) was seen standing by Queen's Monument.*

Left: *When Maidstone bought its Lilac Leopards from Nottingham City Transport in 1977 it retained the livery and the fleet number — in this case 20.*

Above: *A substantial proportion of the Maidstone fleet now consists of Bedford YMTs with Allison automatic gearboxes. No 76, delivered in 1979 is one of a batch with Duple 61-seat bodies.*

Centre right: *An all-Leyland Titan PD2/10 of Portsmouth Corporation (68:GTP 985) approaches the Coach and Horses, Hilsea.*

Bottom right: *Photographed at the same point are 311, one of the 15 Burlingham-bodied BUT trolleybuses delivered in 1950-51 and, in the background, a Southdown all-Leyland PD2/1 on 39, the ex-Denmead Queen route from Hambledon.*

25 SEA FRONT SERVICE
CLARENCE PIER

WHEELERS
FOR
TIMBER
LEADING D.I.Y.
SPECIALISTS
36 SOUTHAMPTON
WHEELERS
FOR
TIMBER
BUILDERS
SUPPLIES
PLEASE PAY
AS YOU ENTER
3221
221 BTP

Left: *Still at work in 1971 was Portsmouth No 5 a Leyland Titan TD4 converted to open top and dating from 1935.*

Bottom left: *The first Atlanteans arrived in 1963. They had Weymann bodies and totalled 35. Twelve years later one of them was in Southampton on hire to Hants & Dorset.*

Above: *Portsmouth has been one of very few operators to use the Leyland Atlantean in a single-deck version and with Seddon bodywork. 189 (RTP 189J) is seen at the Guildhall with the new civic building under construction in the background.*

Centre right: *Later single-deckers have been Leyland Nationals, one of which is seen passing a Leyland Titan PD2/12 with Metro-Cammell bodywork converted to open top.*

Bottom right: *Alexander bodywork is fitted to this Atlantean AN68/IR seen at The Hard in 1975, some four years before the new bus station was built there.*

BAYLIS SUPERMARKETS
PLUS GREEN SHIELD STAMPS
217
STATIONS
91
ERD160

BUTLERS
WHERE MEN SHOP
WHITLEY WOOD
121
ARD 684

Left: *Reading for many years used only lowbridge bodywork so far as double-deckers were concerned and this all-Crossley DD42/8, one of 12 delivered in 1950, was no exception.*

Bottom left: *With the exception of the first six experimental trolleybuses delivered to Reading in 1936 which were lowbridge, all the rest were highbridge. 121, a Park Royal-bodied AEC 661T, was one of 25 which made possible withdrawal of the trams in 1939.*

Right: *Park Royal bodywork was fitted also to this AEC Regent III of 1946 seen at Reading stations some 18 years after its delivery in 1956.*

Centre right: *Burlingham bodies were fitted to the last batch of Reading trolleybuses which entered service in 1961 and were withdrawn eight years later. They were Sunbeam F4As. Behind 190 is 171, a Sunbeam S7/Park Royal dating from 1950.*

Below: *With the delivery of eight Dennis Loline IIIs in 1962 highbridge motorbuses appeared in the Reading motorbus fleet for the first time. 42 and 40 were in the second batch — of 10 — delivered two years later. Bodywork was East Lancs.*

22
HORNCASTLE
225
225
PAY AS YOU ENTER
25 DP

35
Westwood Glen
CIRCULAR
APPOINTMENTS
40 WEST ST READING
151
PAY AS YOU ENTER
mcw
WRD 151T

Top left: *AEC Reliances were the usual single-deck purchases from 1957 to 1965 and 225 (originally 25) with Duple Northern bodywork — earlier ones had been Burlingham — is typical.*

Left: *Batches of Bristol VRTs and Metropolitans have been followed by Metrobuses and Leyland Titans and 151, one of the former is seen in July, 1979.*

Above: *Rather unusually for municipal undertakings Southampton retained smaller types of vehicle in the shape of Leyland Cubs with Park Royal bodies. 53 (OW 7315) was delivered in 1935 and served through the war.*

Below: *In the latter part of the war and until 1955 all new buses for Southampton were Guy Arabs mostly with Gardner 6LW engines and, with five exceptions in 1944, carrying Park Royal bodywork. 203 was a 1950 delivery.*

SWAYTHLING
250
JOW 923

P&O Normandy Ferries
5
Swaythling
via Bassett
7
100
BOW 507C

Left: *250, a Guy Arab UF, with 36 seats and room for 18 standing, was one of the last of the make placed in service by Southampton. The chassis was new in 1952 but the Park Royal body was not built until 1955.*

Bottom left: *From 1962 to 1967 there were deliveries of AEC Regent Vs. 371 and 377, both with East Lancs bodies date from 1965 and 1966 respectively. The former was renumbered 100 in 1979 to mark the centenary of public transport in Southampton and painted in the prewar livery.*

Top right: *The first AEC Swift for Southampton was Strachans-bodied No 1 seen in Pound Tree Road during its first week in service in 1967.*

Centre right: *The type of rear-engined double-decker adopted was the Leyland Atlantean. One of the more recent, 238 has East Lancs bodywork.*

Bottom right: *When photographed in 1978 Southend Transport 316, a Leyland Titan PD3/6 with Massey bodywork was in its last few weeks of operation as the undertaking's last lowbridge bus. Its use on service 12 was very unusual. It had been operating since 1958.*

EAST CIRCULAR
63A
BAXTERS Jewellers
130
SOUTHEND CORPORATION TRANSPORT
W.A. LAYZELL

LEIGH CHURCH
25
SOUTHEND TRANSPORT
205
VDB 915

Left: *The Southend trolleybuses were withdrawn in 1954. 130, with austerity bodywork by Strachans was an AEC dating from 1948.*

Bottom left: *Originally North Western Road Car and later Selnec PTE this 1962 Leyland Leopard subsequently became Southend 205.*

Right: *A new Leopard for Southend in 1976 was 202 with Plaxton Elite Express body.*

Centre right: *As might be expected Southend operates open top services and a typical conversion is this converted Leyland Titan PD3/6 with Massey bodywork. It was new as a covered top in 1958.*

Below: *In 1966 Southend bought five Leyland Royal Tiger Worldmasters with Weymann bodywork which had previously been in the Glasgow fleet. 212 was one of these.*

Above: *Adequate indicators are Southend practice as evidenced by 215, a Leyland Leopard of 1968.*

Below: *Southend 389, a 1975 Daimler Fleetline after the fitting of a curved windscreen. The vehicle is seen in Southend central bus station.*

# National Bus Company Subsidiaries

As indicated in the introductory chapter, there have been some considerable changes in the organisation of NBC subsidiary companies in the traffic areas. These had, indeed, been preceded by some readjustment which followed the division of the Tilling and British Automobile Traction interests between Thomas Tiling and British Electric Traction in 1942. Almost all the companies had been Tilling & BAT with, of course, a substantial railway interest but Eastern National was a Tilling company. The 1942 rearrangement left Aldershot & District, East Kent, Maidstone & District and Southdown as companies in the BET sphere and Eastern Counties, Eastern National, Hants & Dorset, Southern Vectis, Thames Valley and Wilts & Dorset with Tilling Motor Services. This was to have some effect upon vehicle ordering policy where managerial matters had previously been a matter for BET guidance but the postwar demand for vehicles of any kind almost regardless of type made this less obvious than it might otherwise have been.

Below: *A 1939 Bristol K5G of the Bristol Omnibus Co Ltd which was rebodied in 1950 and bought by Eastern Counties in 1959 to replace elderly rebodied Leyland Titans.*

After the decision of BET in 1968 to sell its British bus interests to the British Transport Commission and the consequent establishment of the National Bus Company further consolidation was carried out. Southdown took over first the management and later the operations of the Brighton, Hove & District Omnibus Co Ltd, the heir to the Thomas Tilling Brighton operations and a more substantial partner than Southdown in the pooling arrangement with Brighton Corporation. The red BH&D livery gradually disappeared and, as the corporation had changed from red to blue to achieve differentiation from the company, the area lost its red buses completely.

Another red to vanish was that of Westcliff-on-Sea Motor Services which had been a Tilling company since 1935 and was absorbed by Eastern National. Rather unexpectedly Hants & Dorset long a 'green' operator went red after it had absorbed Wilts & Dorset while the merger of the Thames Valley and Aldershot & District concerns as the Thames Valley and Aldershot Omnibus Co. Ltd with the fleetname Alder Valley. Adjustments have been made in operating areas and there was at one time an extension of joint through service arrangements but these have tended to diminish as service prunings have become necessary. East Kent withdrew from the Hastings area and Maidstone & District from Ashford and Faversham garages while it also reduced its operation around Gravesend and Sevenoaks. Alder Valley is now seen regularly in Southampton while Eastern National has relinquished certain routes in favour of independents. Fleets have been reduced in size particularly those required for day excursions and tours operation.

Below: *One of 20 Leyland Titan PD1As with ECW bodywork which Eastern Counties placed in service in 1947 and withdrew in 1963. It is seen on Hall Quay, Great Yarmouth.*

Right: *Originally a Bristol K6A with Park Royal highbridge austerity body in 1944, Eastern Counties LK147 was converted to K5G in 1953 when it also received an 8ft wide lowbridge ECW body.*

Bottom right: *The relatively flat nature of its territory has always inclined the ECOC to favour lower-powered vehicles. The third prototype Bristol SC was its LC501, an SC4LK with 35-seat body.*

BRADWELL
GORLESTON WHITE HORSE
SHRUBLANDS
19
Silk Cut. the mild cigarette
FAH 103

33A SERVICE
PAY AS YOU ENTER
TVF 501

Top: *Two of the seven Eastern Counties Leyland Leopards with Alexander dual purpose bodywork seating 49 in Surrey Street garage, Norwich.*

Above: *Seen in Norwich in 1973 VR31B is one of the Bristol VRTs received from the Scottish Bus Group — this one came from Western SMT — in exchange for Bristol Lodekkas.*

Above: *Hired by Eastern Counties from Western National in 1978 was this open-top Bristol LDL seen on the seafront service at Felixstowe.*

221 EAST BERGHOLT
EASTERN COUNTIES
PAY AS YOU ENTER
TCL 139R

SOUTHEND
GOOD FOOD
NORWICH SOUTHEND
RLE 863
PAY AS YOU ENTER
BRISTOL RE
WNG 863H

Left: *A 1977 Bristol LH6P of Eastern Counties (LH919) which was allocated to the East Bergholt outstation of Ipswich garage when new. It frequently worked the last journey daily on the 207 service from Colchester.*

Bottom left: *A dual-purpose Bristol RE in Colchester on the Norwich-Southend express service in the summer of 1970.*

Right: *A prewar Eastern National Leyland Titan TD4 which entered service in 1937, was rebodied in 1949 and was not withdrawn until 1964.*

Below: *Long service was given also by this 1948 Bristol K5G which entered the Westcliff fleet in 1948, passed with the business to Eastern National and was withdrawn in 1966, two years after it was photographed in Little Clacton.*

Left: *With the disbanding of National Travel (South East) this 1974 Plaxton-bodied Bristol RELH6L passed to Eastern National. It is seen in London outside the Heymarket Theatre.*

Centre left: *The purchase of Moore Bros (Kelvedon) in 1963 brought with it a number of Guy Arab double-deckers including 2012, a Massey-bodied Arab IV dating from 1958.*

Below: *During 1978 Eastern National withdrew Leyland National 1703 from normal service, numbered it 9015 in the service vehicle fleet and painted it in blue drivers' training livery.*

Right: *Outside Braintree depot in 1971 stand 1411, a dual-purpose Bristol MW5G, 2824, a Bristol FLF6G, and 1324 another MW5G with bus bodywork.*

Bottom right: *Seen at Eight Ash Green, near Colchester, in 1978 is Eastern National 1205, a Bedford YMT with Duple Dominant II 53-seat body in dual-purpose livery. It was the first coach allocated to Colchester for four years.*

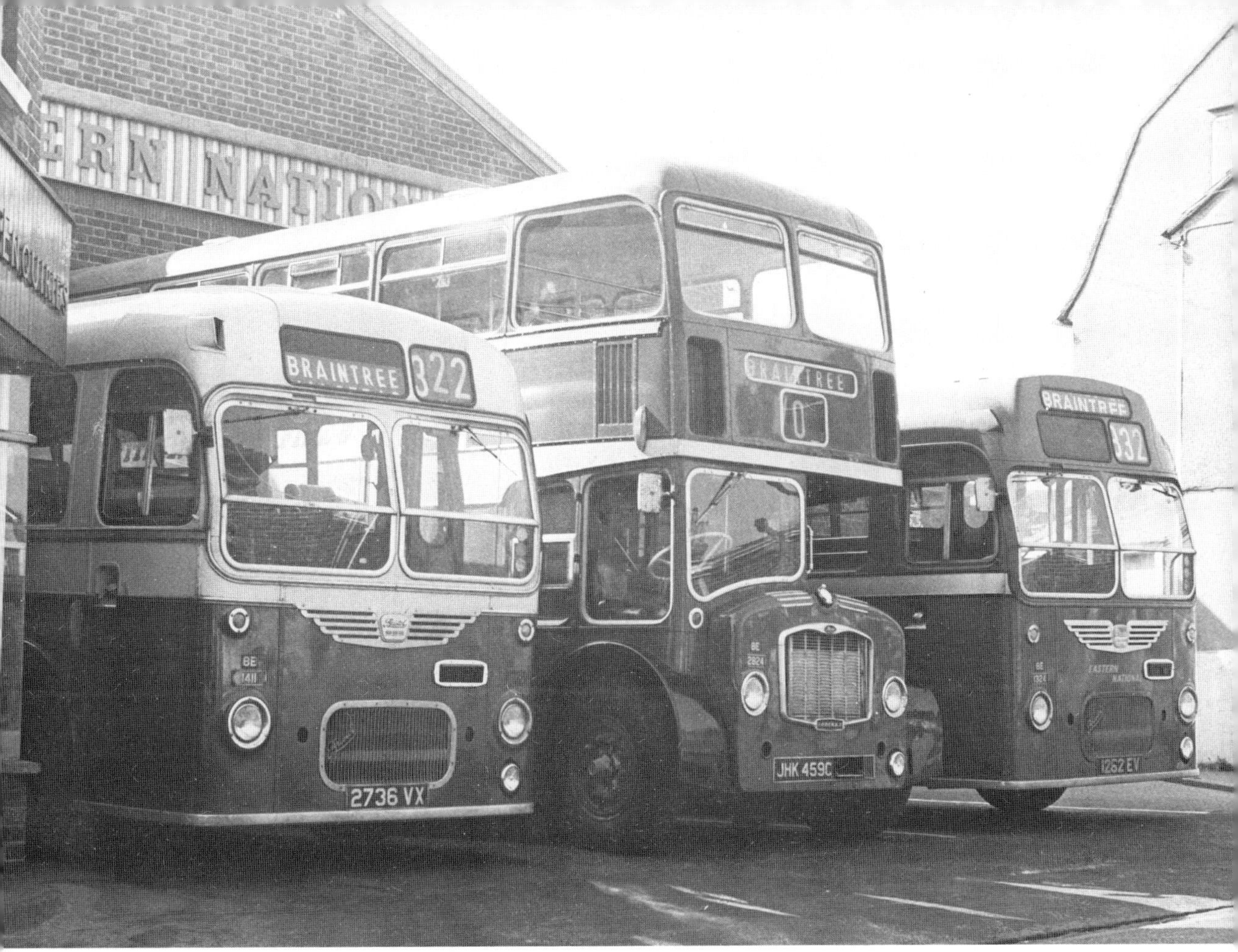

EASTERN NATIONAL
ENQUIRIES
BRAINTREE 322
BRAINTREE
BRAINTREE 332
2736 VX
JHK 459C
1262 EV

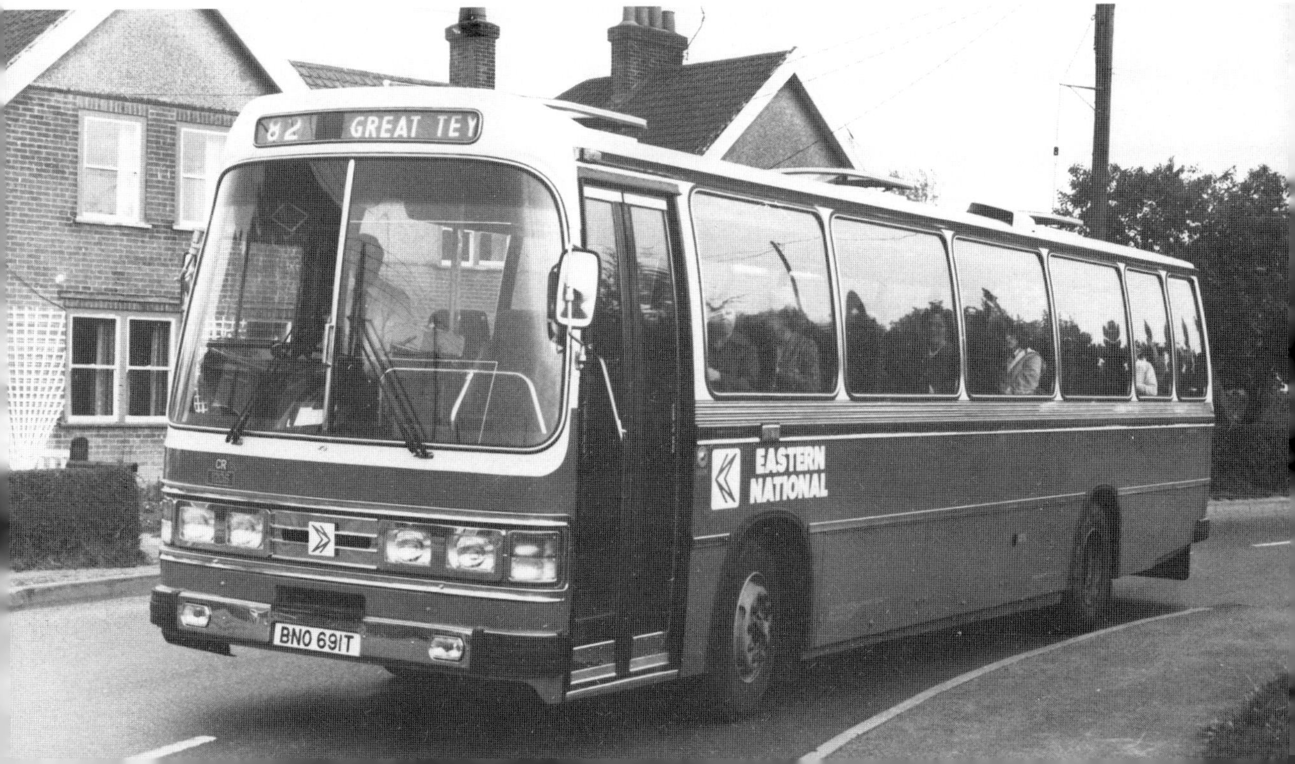

82 GREAT TEY
EASTERN NATIONAL
BNO 691T

118 HARWICH Bus Station
117 HARWICH Bus Station
MAR 783P
LJN 663P
LEYLAND NATIONAL

LONDON
151
WVX 529F

*Left: A pair of Leyland Nationals takes its layover at Harwich with the old lighthouse in the background.*

*Bottom left: Eastern National is now one of the few operators of a regular headway double-deck service to London. Before the present Bristol VRTs there were the Lodekkas.*

*Below: One of the main features of the postwar operations of East Kent Road Car was the opening of new bus stations such as those at Canterbury and Folkestone. The latter was opened in 1955.*

Left: *The effects of the war are apparent in this view of the damaged Dover garage with Tilling-Stevens and Dennis Lancet buses.*

Centre left: *An East Kent Guy Arab with utility body on a city service in Canterbury. The company took delivery mainly of this make of double deckers from 1944 to 1957.*

Below: *A prewar Leyland Titan with postwar ECW body operating on another Canterbury city service.*

Right: *A revamped Dennis Lancet 3 stands beside a Weymann-bodied AEC Reliance. The latter types was destined to be used extensively from 1955 onwards.*

Bottom right: *A 1962 Reliance entering Victoria Coach Station 10 years later with a new Plaxton Panorama Elite body.*

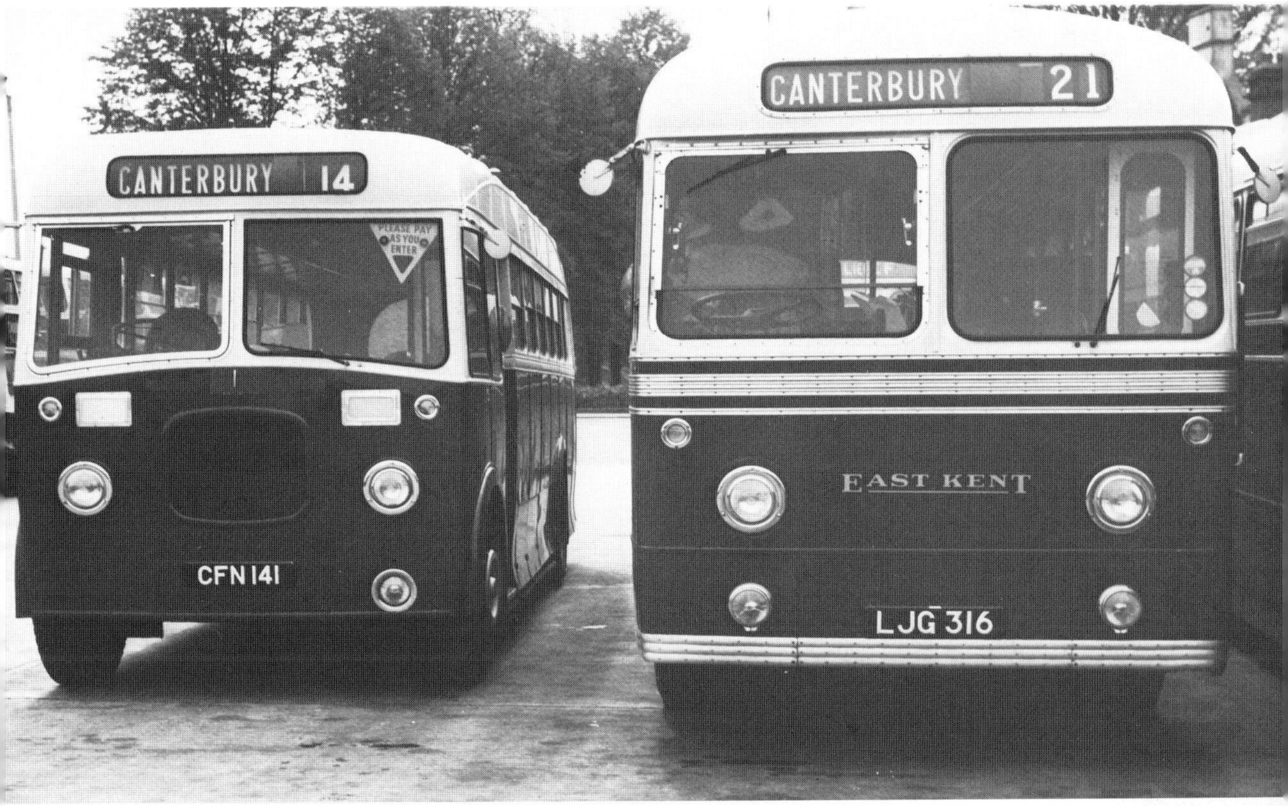

CANTERBURY 14
CFN 141
CANTERBURY 21
EAST KENT
LJG 316

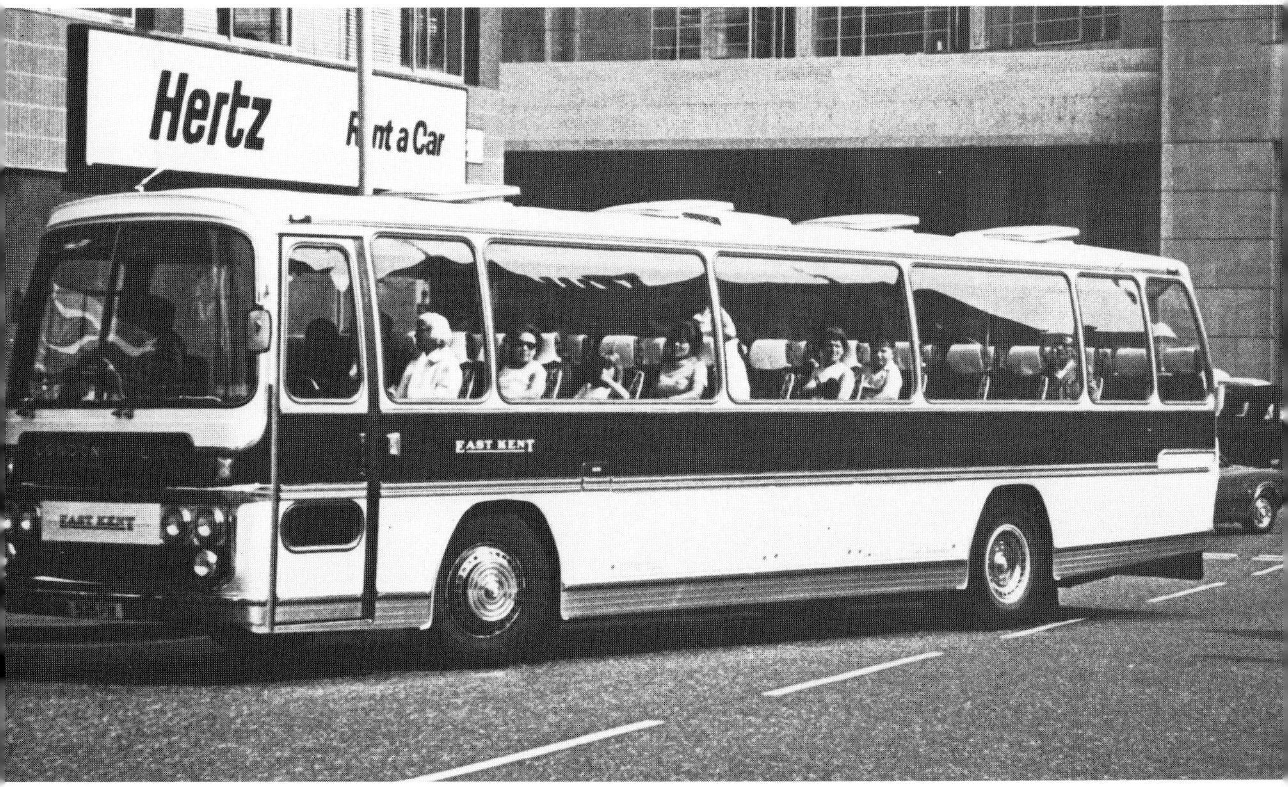

Hertz
Rent a Car
EAST KENT
EAST KENT

PRIVATE
EAST KENT
GFN 920
London via Epsom

BANK
DEAL
90
ST. MARGARET'S BAY
DOVER, CAPEL
6786 FN

Top left: *An East Kent Guy Arab IV converted to open-top is seen at the Derby.*

Left: *AEC Regent Vs are dwindling in numbers but they were for nearly 20 years a familiar feature in East Kent. They had Park Royal bodies and this one was delivered in 1963.*

Above: *Leyland Nationals have invaded East Kent as they have most parts of England and Wales and 1086 is seen on a Canterbury city service.*

Right: *In the autumn of 1979 a Willowbrook-bodied Bristol VRT in Mill Street, Maidstone, on the service from Folkestone operated jointly with Maidstone & District.*

Bottom right: *One of four Plaxton-bodied Ford R1014s delivered to East Kent in 1977 is seen on an Ashford local service.*

Above: *Hants & Dorset as one of the Tilling and BAT companies to come under the Tilling regime became a Bristol user. In due course it operated the last lowbridge Bristols in public service. They were actually KSWs from the absorbed Wilts & Dorset.*



Below: *Built in 1953 this Bristol LS6B spent some 14 years with Southern Vectis before it was moved to the mainland to work for Hants & Dorset at Southampton*

Above: *Typical of the H&D Bristol Lodekkas is this FS6G (1414) seen in Christchurch in 1971 some nine years after it entered service.*

Below: *Following the takeover of the King Alfred routes at Winchester some withdrawn H&D buses were relicensed to take over operations. They included Bristol KSW 1361 here seen at Teg Down on an ex-KA service.*

17
Broadway
Worthy Road
SPRINGVALE
17
National Bus
- together we're going places!
HANTS & DORSET
WCG 106

POOLE
1
COME IN FROM
OUT OF TOWN
ARNDALE CENTRE Poole
DAIMLER
HANTS & DORSET
HANTS & DORSET
VRU 127J

Left: *The last bus to retain King Alfred livery was AEC/Park Royal Bridgemaster WCG 106 which became 2201 in the H&D fleet. It is seen here on its final day of operation — 29 November 1975 — when it was used for a special tour with old KA blinds.*

Bottom left: *New in the summer of 1971 H&D Roe-bodied Daimler Fleetline 1904 had been ordered by Gosport & Fareham with five others but all were diverted to Hants & Dorset and allocated to Poole.*

Right: *3534, one of H&D's 1974 Bristol LH6Ls aboard the Sandbanks ferry on its way from Bournemouth to Swanage.*

Centre right: *Originally numbered 3010 but, by then, 1515, a Willowbrook-bodied Bedford VAM70 is seen working for Hants & Dorset in Swanage in the autumn of 1971.*

Below: *Working a local route at Lymington in the spring of 1977 was 2001, an Alexander-bodied Ford A type seen at the Town Station.*

uestaff staff agency
48 HIGH STREET
STREET FAREHAM TEL 4711
8
DEUTZ
Provincial
HOR 676E

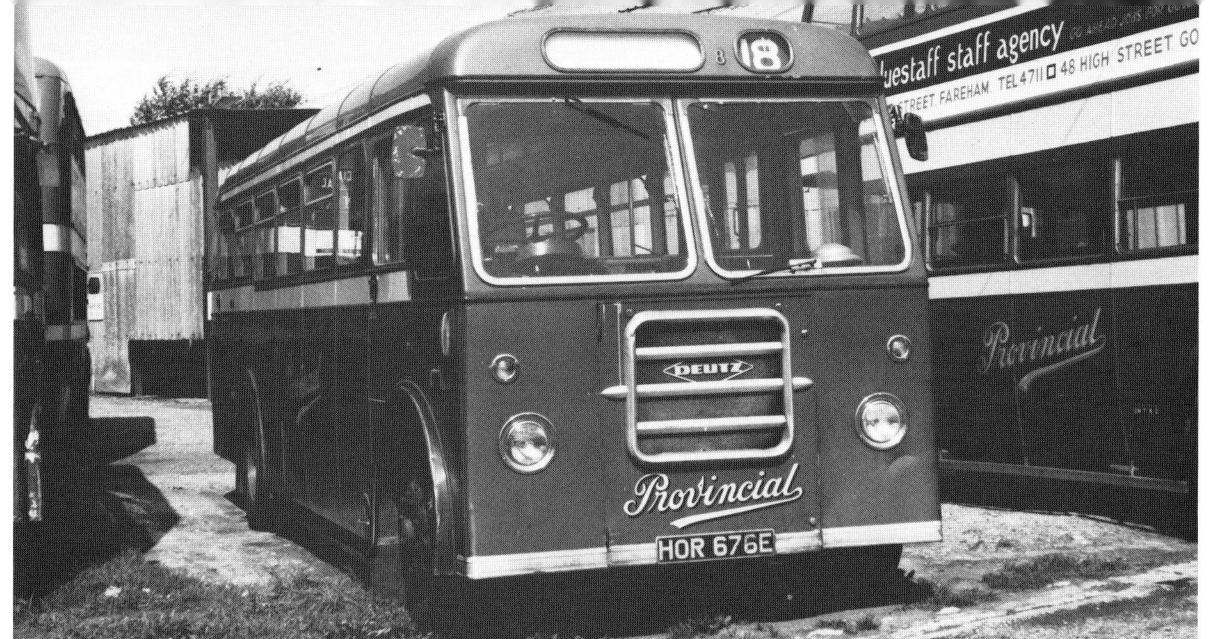

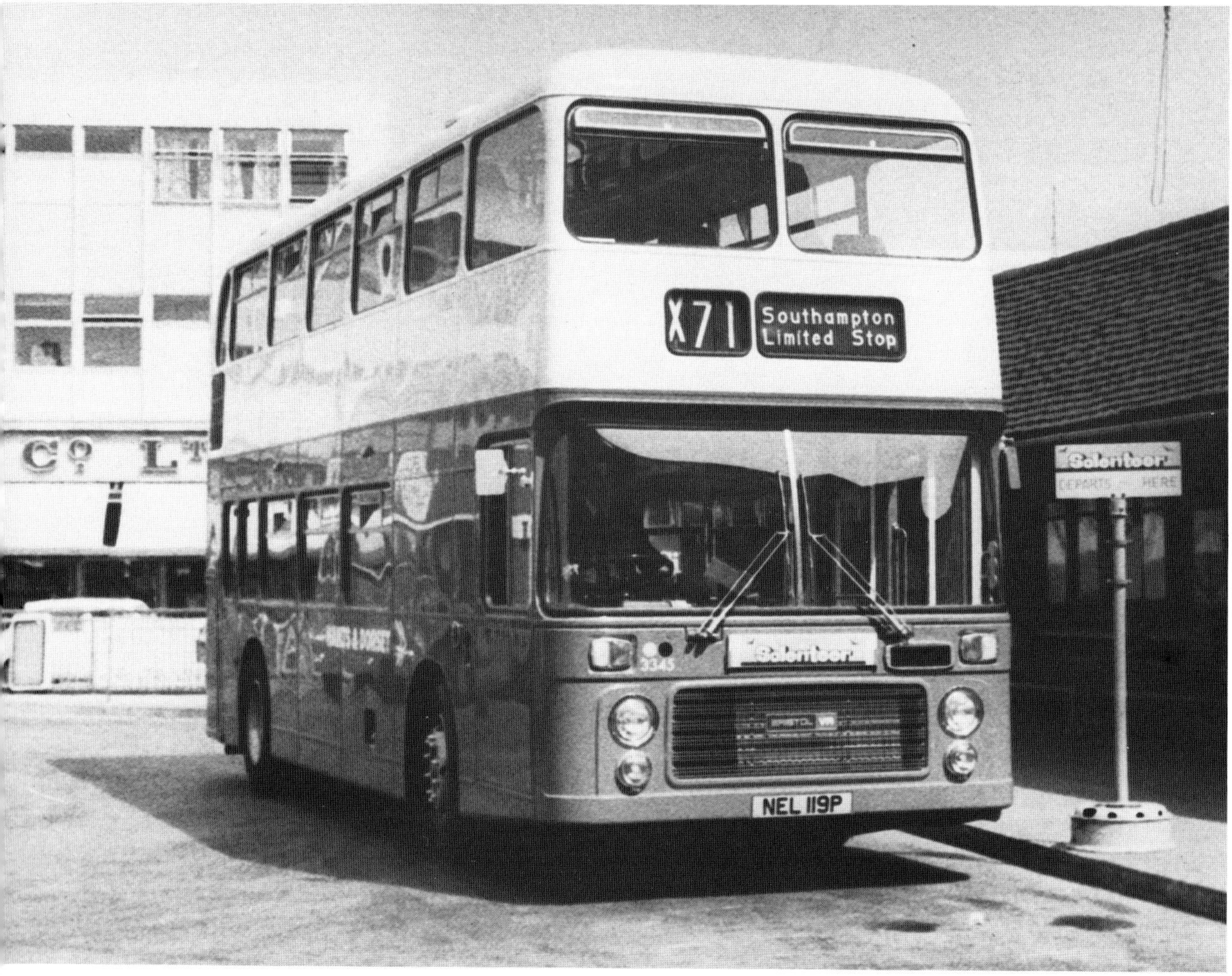
X71
Southampton
Limited Stop
NEL 119P
3345

Top left: *In 1967 Gosport & Fareham introduced a single-deck Guy rebuilt Arab III with air-cooled Deutz engine and a Reading 41-passenger body — 14 standing. It was intended for the Fareham-Knowle route and most of the 192,000 miles which it operated during its five-years life were accumulated thereon. Seen in its original livery as No 8 in 1970 it later became 37 with more cream round its windows.*

Left: *When Hants & Dorset and Southdown introduced the joint limited-stop service between Southampton and Southsea as* The Solenter *the H&D journeys were worked with new ECW-bodied dual-purpose Bristol VRTs. 3345 is seen in Fareham bus station.*

Above: *Surplus Southdown Leyland Leopards have passed to a number of operators, both NBC and independent. This Marshall-bodied example was one of two which reached Gosport & Fareham by way of Hants & Dorset in 1972.*

Right: *In 1938 Maidstone & District took delivery of 12 Bristol K5Gs on which were placed two-years old Weymann lowbridge bodies off Bristol GO5Gs delivered two years earlier. The latter were returned to Bristol, received new bodies and used for Bath tramway replacement. K5G No 279 is seen at Sevenoaks.*

Bottom right: *A similar fate befell four GO5Gs with highbridge Weymann bodies in the Chatham & District fleet including 355 seen at Chatham Town Hall. Behind it is 392, a 1931 Leyland Titan which outlasted most of its contemporaries in C&D service.*

SCOUT MOTOR Co
DAY TOUR
DAY TOUR
NKK 831
DKP 973

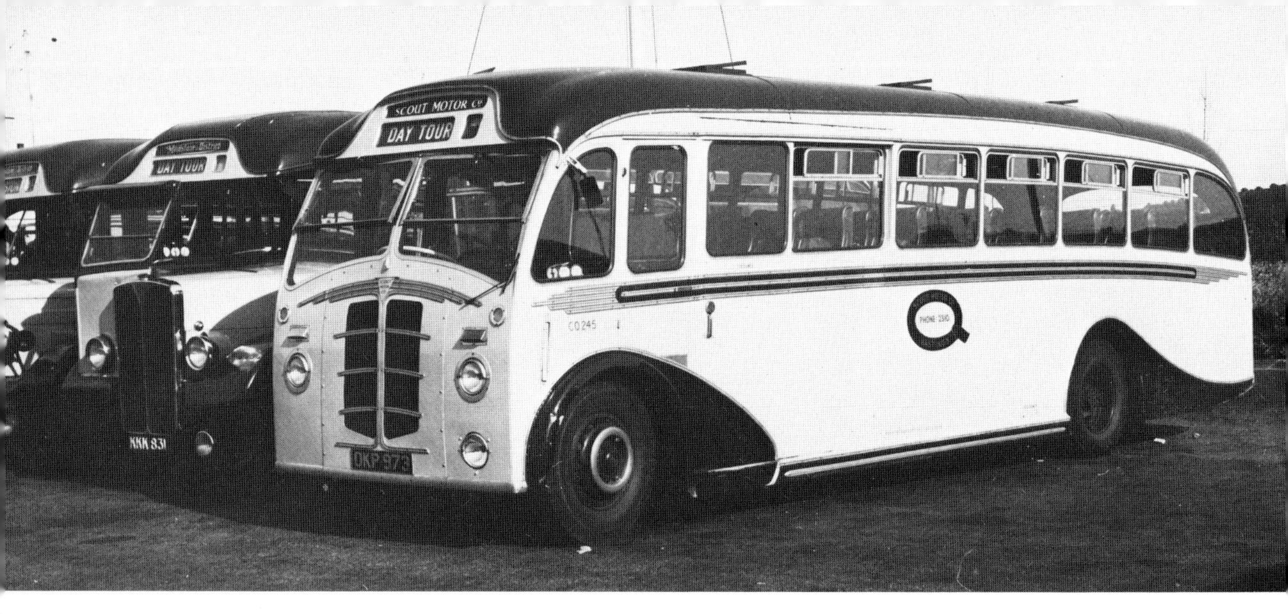

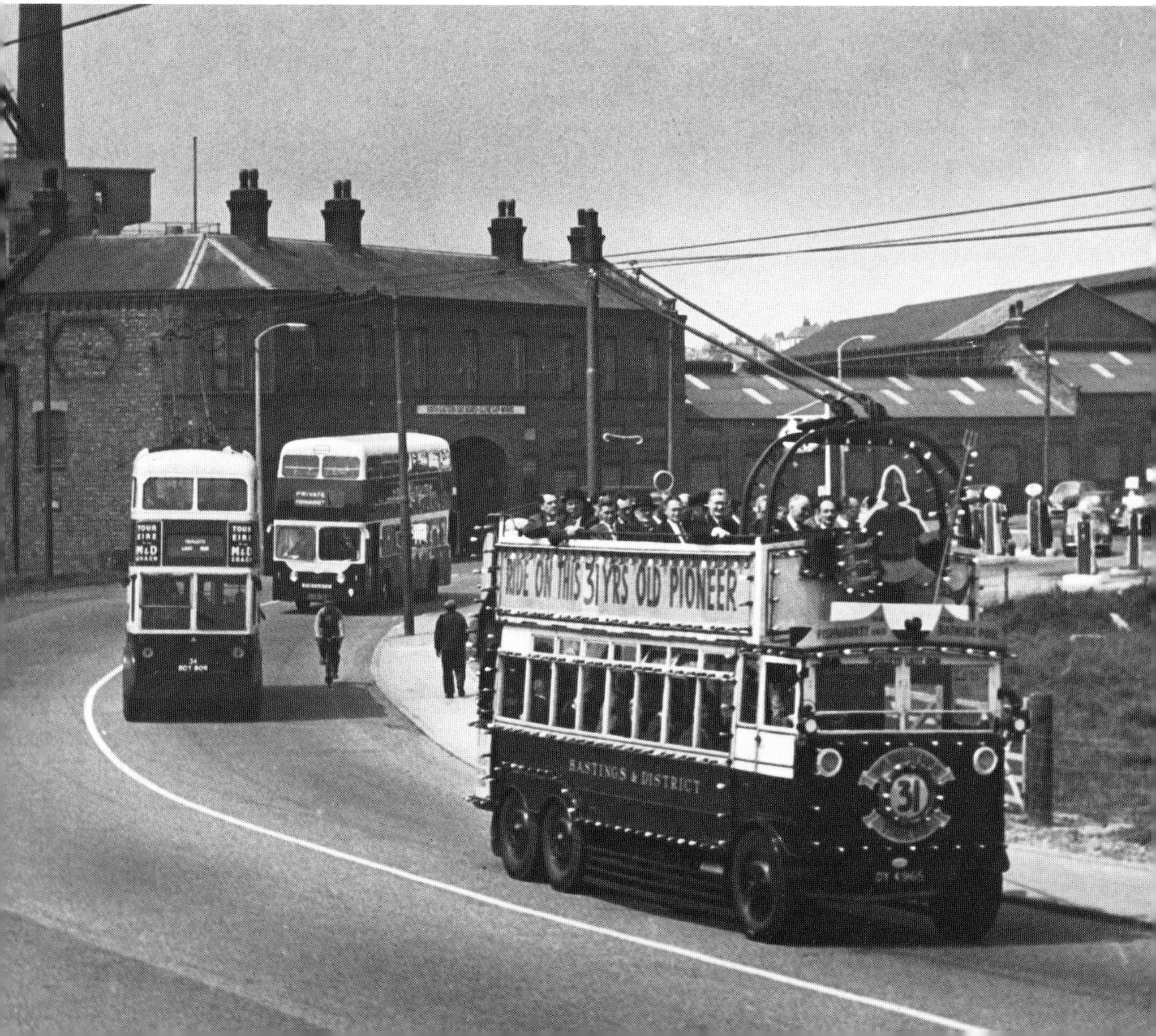
RIDE ON THIS 31 YRS OLD PIONEER
HASTINGS & DISTRICT
31
M&D
M&D

Top left: *A shortage of new chassis led to the ordering from John C. Beadle, of Dartford of semi-chassisless coaches using engines and other parts of withdrawn prewar vehicles. Among the BET companies which did this were East Kent, Maidstone & District, Potteries and Southdown. This M&D example was numbered CO245 and is seen at Folkestone in the livery of the Scout Motor Company, Hastings, which had been acquired but had had its livery retained for some vehicles.*

Left: *The Hastings trolleybus abandonment with the subsequently preserved Guy six-wheeler, Sunbeam trolleybus 34 and one of the lowheight Leyland Atlanteans which replaced the trolleybuses.*

Above: *Park Royal bodywork was relatively rare so far as M&D vehicles were concerned but it was fitted to eight lowbridge and 14 highbridge AEC Regent Vs built in 1956. One of the latter type is seen at Tunbridge Wells War Memorial together with two Bristol K6As and, rear view, one of the 11 integral Harrington-Commer Contenders bought in 1955.*

Centre right: *In 1960 Maidstone & District purchased 15 Albion Nimbus/Harrington seating 30 for use on light traffic routes and 3312 — originally S312 — is seen at Tunbridge Wells Central station on the Burwash route initiated by Redcar and now abandoned.*

Bottom right: *AEC Reliant 3212 with Weymann body arrives in East Grinstead High Street from Crowborough in 1967. The Crowborough-Hartfield section of the route was originated by Sargents.*

THE GREAT GAS GALA
WEEDS WOOD 142
MAIDSTONE & DISTRICT
SD97
GCN 809G 
5253
182  WEEDS WOOD
DANGER
No Entry
for
Pedestrians
DANGER
No Entry
for
Pedestrians

Left: *M&D single-deck Daimler Fleetlines went to Northern General and from that operator came Leyland Atlanteans with Alexander bodywork looking somewhat unusual in Kent (5007:GCN 809G). It is seen in Chatham.*

Bottom left: *The Medway towns have been serving as a proving ground for comparative tests conducted on behalf of the National Bus Company. In the first series the types involved were Metropolitan, Volvo Ailsa and Bristol VRT. A Metropolitan is seen leaving the modern Pentagon bus station in Chatham. The requirements of the television cameras which scan the station have caused the adoption of the conspicuous roof numbers.*

Right: *One of the Ailsa double-deckers with Alexander bodywork which also participated in the Medway towns tests.*

Below: *A Leyland Panther in Hastings in the autumn of 1972 wearing NBC green and white livery but still carrying the old style fleetname.*

Above: *For a period the Maidstone-Hastings service was single-deck operated, usually by dual-purpose Leyland Nationals but in 1979 it reverted to double-deck operation with new Bristol VRTs. 5831 is seen in St Leonards.*

Left: *Not many companies operated trolleybuses but Brighton, Hove and District did so under the terms of the Brighton area agreement of 1939. Eight were delivered by 1940 but only went into service after the war. 6344 is seen passing Brighton Racecourse.*

Top right: *A 1939 Leyland Titan TD5 which Southdown had rebodied by Park Royal in 1950 is now preserved and is seen in Arundel conveying enthusiasts.*

Right: *Delivered to Brighton, Hove & District, Southdown Bristol RESL/ECW 2204 stands at Crawley bus station in January 1979 waiting to leave for West Hoathly.*

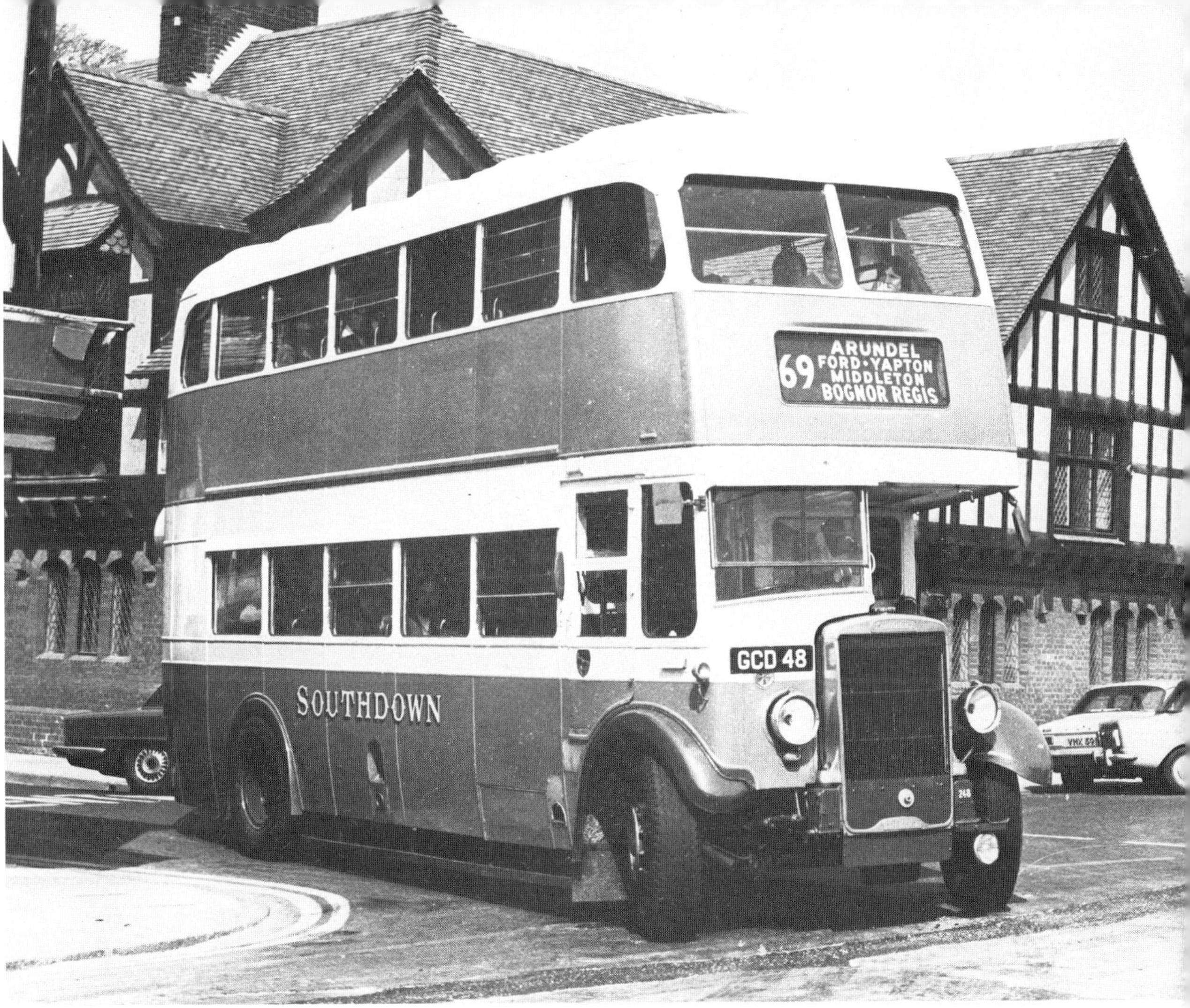

69 ARUNDEL
FORD · YAPTON
MIDDLETON
BOGNOR REGIS
SOUTHDOWN
GCD 48

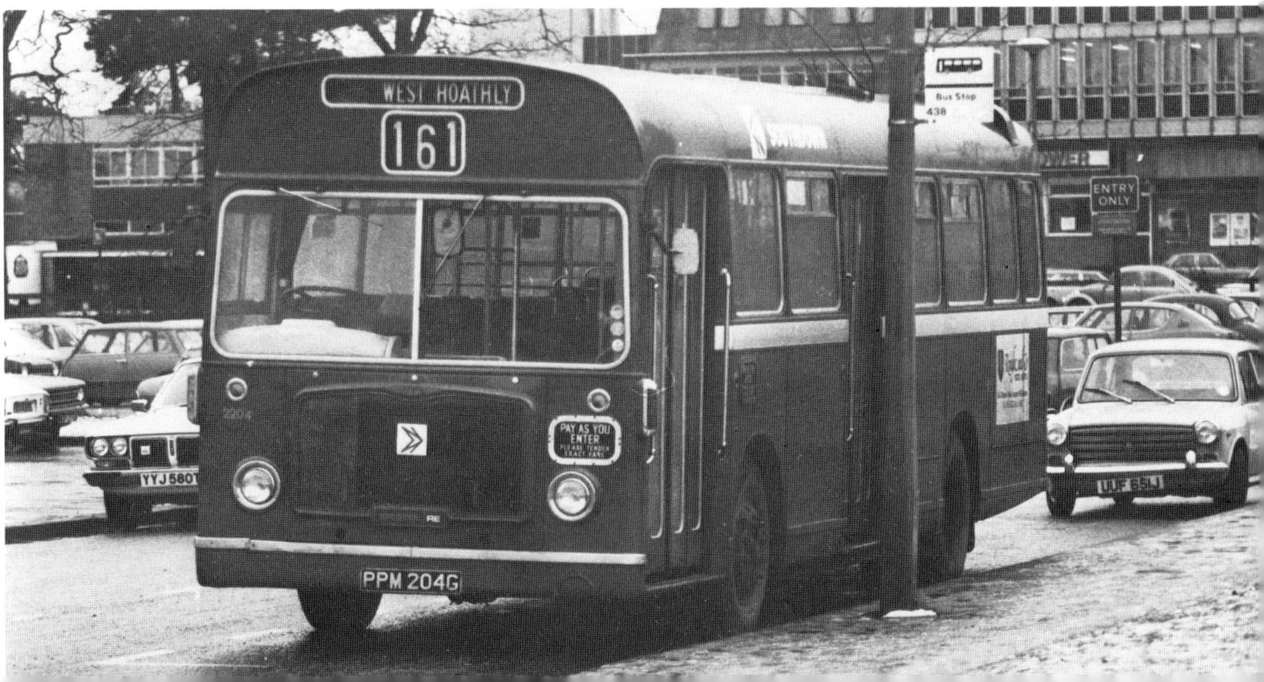

WEST HOATHLY
161
PAY AS YOU
ENTER
PPM 204G
Bus Stop
438
ENTRY
ONLY

WORTHING PIER
230
1820
2073
SOUTHDOWN
FPM 73C
SOUTHDOWN

23A
SOUTHGATE DRIVE
THE BOULEVARD
HANDCROSS
CADETS
TOWN SERVICE
476
7
PUF 631
SOUTHDOWN

Top left: *Whilst most ex-BH&D Bristol Lodekkas were allocated to the Brighton area after the absorption by Southdown, 2073 was sent to Worthing garage whence it often operated back to its old haunts.*

Left: *Southdown took delivery of its last Guy Arabs in 1955-56. One of these 48 Park Royal-bodied vehicles was 521 seen waiting to leave Crawley for Handcross on a service which later passed to London Country.*

Above: *A design and style for long associated with Southdown was the fully fronted Northern Counties body on the Leyland Titan PD chassis. Some were convertible open-toppers. The 1967 batch is exemplified by 365 (HCD 365E) seen leaving Brighton Pool Valley for Seaford.*

Right: *Brighton, Hove & District 433, a Bristol KSW6B/Eastern Coach Works 60-seater delivered in 1952 in Queen's Road, Brighton.*

Cover yourself with Pearl Unit Funds
assurance
5 PATCHAM
SOUTHDOWN
666
AAP 666T
3A
ORES

32 FLETCHING
HORSTED KEYNES
HAYWARDS HEATH
BRIGHTON
JOBS?
K
KENT
LUF 509
1509

Left: *Not all the newer Bristol VRTs of Southdown are fitted for omo and one such is 666 which entered service in March, 1979 and is seen on a local service in Brighton.*

Bottom left; *East Lancs-bodied Leyland Royal Tiger 1509 about to leave Uckfield for Brighton in 1967. 32, a postwar service, later succumbed to loss of rural traffic.*

Right: *A bleak Boxing Day scene at Church Norton as Southdown 390, an ECW-bodied Daimler Fleetline proceeds from Chichester towards Selsey.*

Below: *Leyland Tiger Cub 638 with Duple bodywork is seen in East Grinstead on 87, a route taken over from East Grinstead Coaches (Sargent).*

GREY-GREEN
NATIONAL
GB

3   PRIVATE
NATIONAL
SOUTHDOWN
SCD 32N

Top left: *New to Southdown in 1961 this Harrington-bodied Leyland Leopard passed later to Tilling which reseated it from ex-East Kent Park Royal dual-purpose vehicles which had been rebodied by Plaxton. 8737 CD is seen in Baldock on hire to Grey-Green having been lent earlier to Black & White and subsequently to Oxford-South Midland.*

Left: *In the 1970s Southdown bought 40 Ford coaches and two are seen here at Brighton racecourse on a private hire job.*

Above: *After the official opening of Newport bus station in 1957, most of the Southern Vectis buses to be seen from the roof of the office block were Bristol Lodekkas, 87 of which were delivered between 1954 and 1965.*

Right: *Some of the Lodekkas were later converted to open top and the old 542 is seen between Ventnor and Shanklin as OT2 in the summer of 1973.*

Above: *More remarkable as an open-top is this 1939 Bristol K5G seen here in 1972 waiting to leave Shanklin for Sandown but still in summer service in 1980.*

Left: *Southern Vectis 564, typical ECW-bodied Bristol RELL leaves Ryde Esplande for Ventnor soon after entering service.*

Top right: *Another Newport bus station view but this time in 1977 shows one of 13 Bristol FLFs delivered in 1964-65 (609) and Bristol VRT 651 then a matter of months old.*

Right: *Restrictive road widths resulted in Southern Vectis buying Marshall-bodied Bristol LHs, one of which — 835 — is here seen at Newport.*

Above: *Leyland Nationals had reached the Isle of Wight by 1973 and Southern Vectis 875 is passing through Godshill Village on a summer evening.*

Left: *Aldershot & District had a tendency towards having odd men out in its fleet and one of these was No 186, a Guy Arab UF with East Lancs body delivered in 1953 and seen in Midhurst in July 1958.*

Bottom left: *Shortage of vehicles led Aldershot & District in 1967 to hire Southdown 1689, an Harrington-bodied Leyland Royal Tiger, which is seen here at Kew Gardens wearing the A&D fleetname on its sides.*

Right: *Following the merging of Aldershot & District with Thames Valley a number of the former's Dennis Lolines was drafted to the latter's depots. MCW-bodied 854 is seen at Maidenhead in April 1974.*

Bottom right: *From 1954 Aldershot & District for some 10 years used the AEC Reliance for single-deck chassis. 284, a Weymann-bodied example delivered in 1957 as 313, is seen in Bradford whither it had conveyed an Omnibus Society party for the last day of trolleybus operation.*

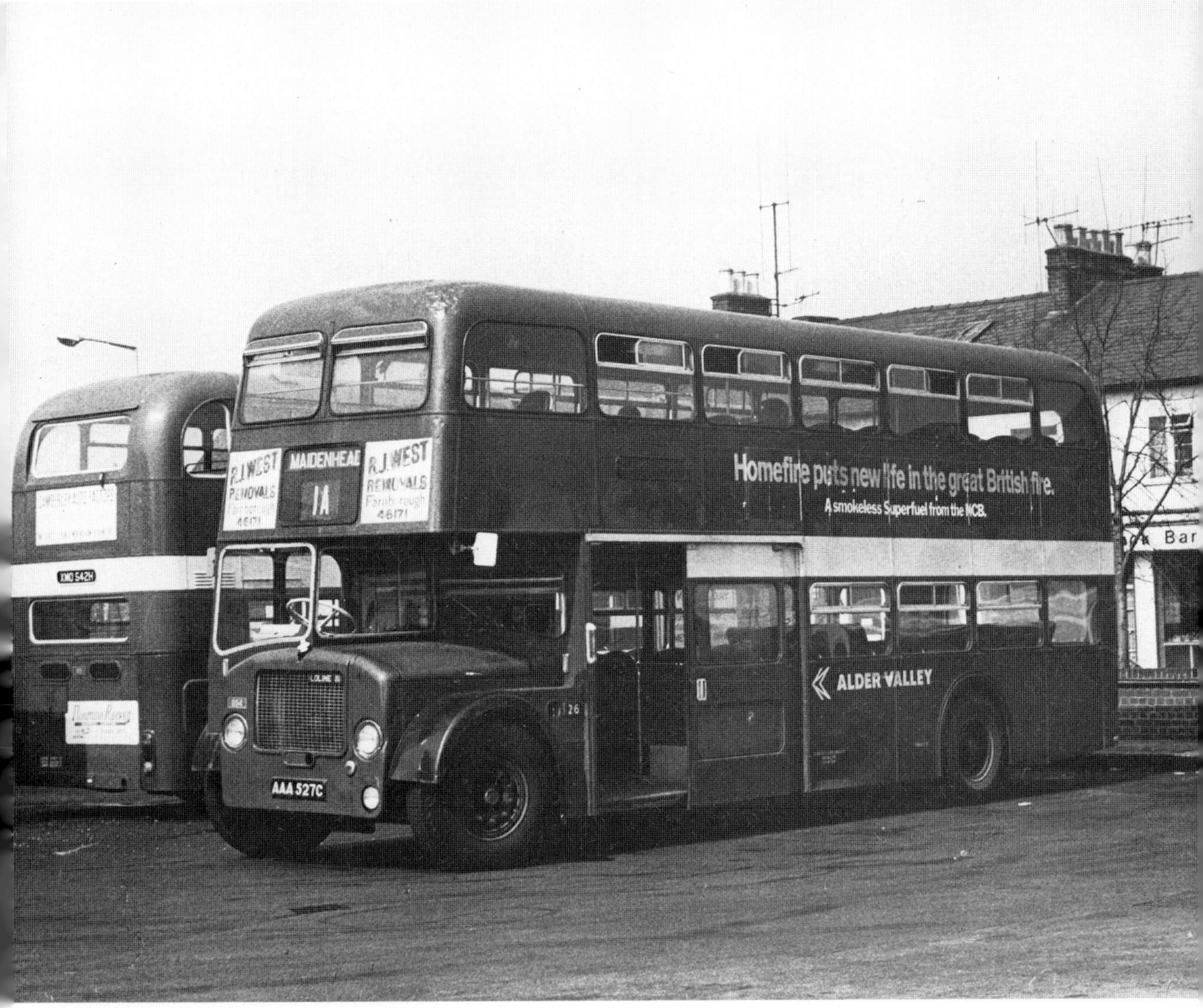
R.J. WEST
REMOVALS
Farnborough
46171
MAIDENHEAD
1A
R.J. WEST
REMOVALS
Farnborough
46171
Homefire puts new life in the great British fire.
A smokeless Superfuel from the NCB.
ALDER VALLEY
AAA 527C
TOUR TO BRADFORD
FOR FINAL TROLLEYBUSES
OMNIBUS
SOCIETY
7
THORNTON ROAD
ALDER VALLEY
ALDER VALLEY
SOU 421

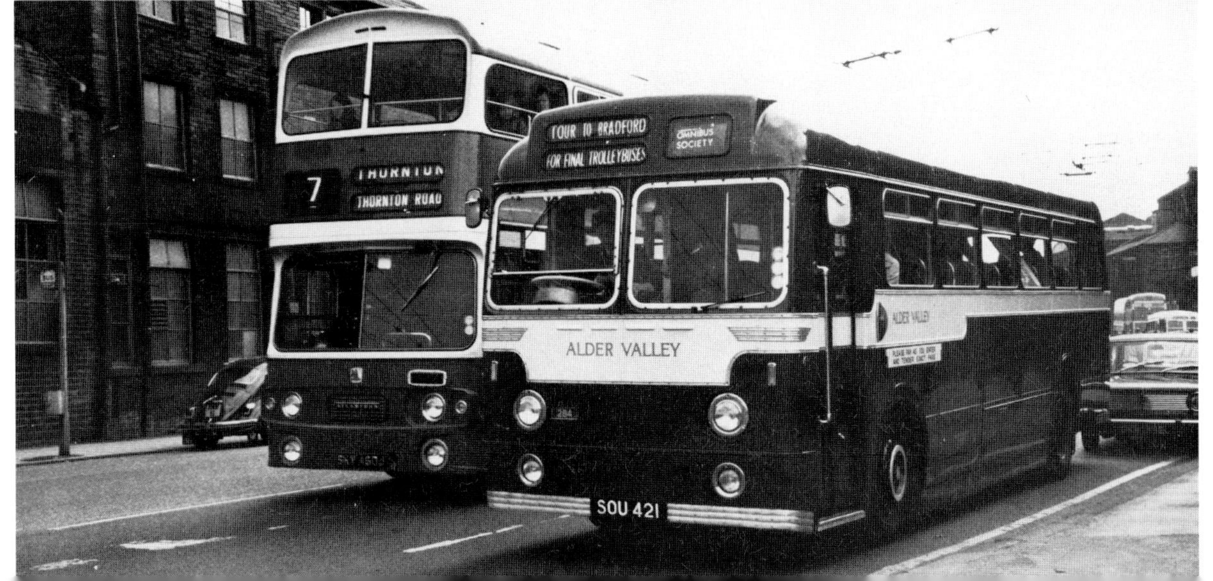

48A
CAMBERLEY
WOKING
649
THE
CURFEW
Except
buses

to enjoy
EVENING
NEWS
more
to
enjoy
EVENING
NEWS
more
to
enjoy
EVENING
NEWS
STRONGS Keg BARLEYCORN
DMO 675

Top left: *Following the Reliances A&D
adopted the Bristol RESL6G. 649, and ECW-
bodied 45-seater is seen at Ottershaw
en route from Chertsey to Camberley via
Woking, a service which ceased as a through
operation on 30 August 1980.*

Left: *Seen after withdrawal from service is
Thames Valley 471, a Bristol K6B built in
1948. With the exception of some Guy Arabs
inherited from Newbury & District almost all
Thames Valley double-deckers were of the
lowbridge type until the advent of the Bristol
Lodekka.*

Above: *This Lodekka was an LD5G out of a
mixed batch of LD5Gs and LD6Gs delivered
to Thames Valley in 1957. It is seen in
Slough.*

Right: *The weight restriction on Marlow
bridge was a problem which haunted Thames
Valley for many years. Indeed it stayed with
Alder Valley for many more. One method of
overcoming it was the use of Bedford OBs
with specially-built Beadle bodies. One of
these is seen just after crossing the bridge in
the spring of 1967.*

Top: *In the 1950s Thames Valley operated a Thameside open-top service between Reading and Maidenhead and an ex-Brighton, Hove & District Bristol K5G is seen crossing Cookham bridge.*

Above: *Dating from 1952 Thames Valley 626, a Bristol LWL6B, is seen at Booker on a local service from High Wycombe in 1966.*

Top right: *One of the Scottish Bus Group Bristol VRTs exchanged for Bristol Lodekkas of NBC companies was previously Western SMT and became Alder Valley 886. It was photographed in Reading.*

Right: *Alder Valley 941, one of the 1977-delivered Bristol VRTs about to leave Onslow Street bus station, Guildford for Winchester on the then newly established through service. On the right a Plaxton-bodied Bedford of Tillingbourne Bus.*

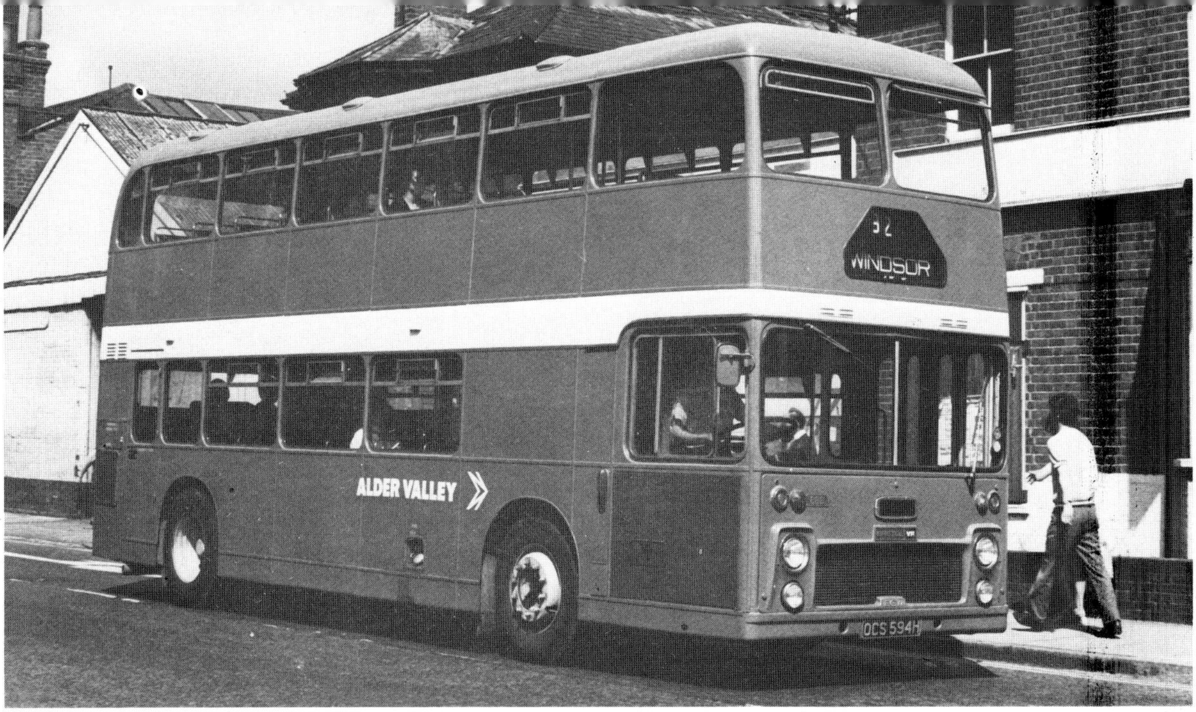

WINDSOR
ALDER VALLEY
OCS 594H

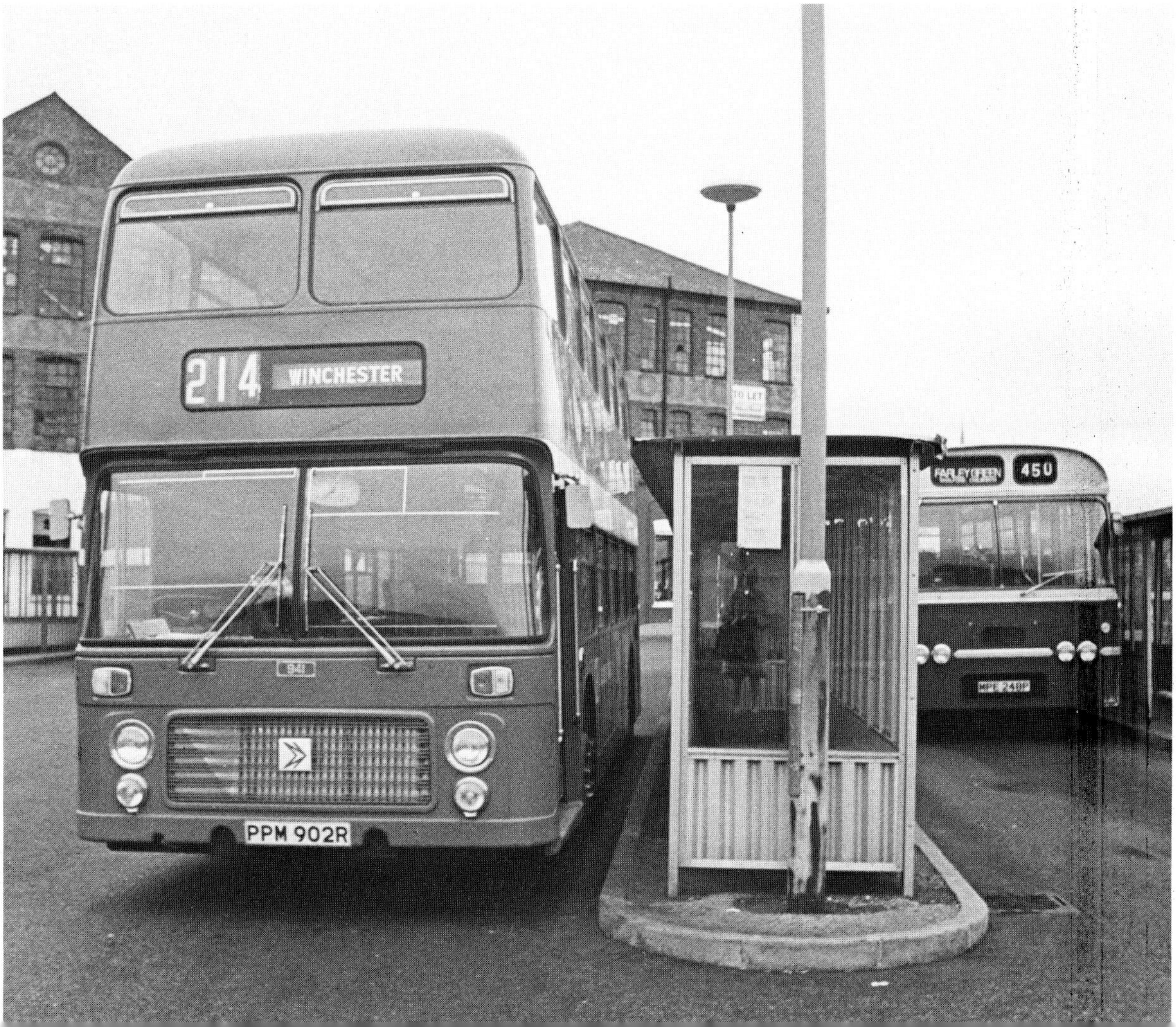

214 WINCHESTER
941
PPM 902R
450
MPE 248P

Above: *At Reading garage in May 1974 are arranged a Bristol RE bus, a Leyland National, a Bedford VAM, a Bristol RE coach, a hired Southend Leyland Leopard, a new Ford R1014 and a Bristol LS.*

Left: *Hired vehicles have made a number of appearances with Alder Valley and an Eastern National Lodekka with Alder Valley fleetname is near East Ilsley in August 1979.*

# South-Eastern Independents

Within the area covered by this book it can reasonably be said that the independents in two parts provide a contrast in themselves.

So far as stage service operation is concerned the south east has long been very sparsely covered. The major companies had long since acquired most of the rivals or potential competitors and even when the Road Traffic Act took effect in 1931 there were relatively few to be found and most of these centred on boundary towns of the company-agreed operating areas such as Guildford and Horsham. The former still retains much of its independent flavour with independents providing town services but the latter has suffered somewhat from the dwindling traffic on rural routes. Three major independents which have gone were almost area companies in their extent. Venture Ltd, of Basingstoke, and Newbury & District Motor Services, which were bought by Red & White in 1945 and 1943 respectively, passed with the rest of R&W bus business to the British Transport Commission in February, 1950. The former came under the aegis of Wilts & Dorset and thereafter, of course, Hants & Dorset while the Newbury & District business went to Thames Valley. The third major business was King Alfred Motor Services operated in and from Winchester by R. Chisnell & Sons Ltd and founded in 1920. Here also the slackening of country bus traffic and reduced demand for town services had its effect and the services were taken over by Hants & Dorset mainly as it was put from a sense of duty.

Below: *Proving perhaps an appropriate transition between NBC companies and independent operators is this Dennis Lancet III with Park Royal bodywork which entered the East Kent fleet in 1950 and was still operating miners services for Thomsett, of Deal, in 1973. It is seen outside the EK Canterbury depot with a party from the M&D and East Kent Bus Club.*

Above: *Postbus operation is relatively scarce in Southern and Eastern England but there are some examples and one of these is the Henley postbus which is seen picking up mail at Greenlands, formerly the home of Lord Hambledon and now the Administrative Staff College.*

Left: *An older postbus service is that in Surrey between Oxted and Lingfield via Tandridge which serves as partial repayment for the East Grinstead-Oxted service withdrawn by London Country. The Commer is seen at The Bell, Old Oxted in 1974.*

Above: *For much of the period covered the independent flag was flown at Winchester by King Alfred Motor Services with a fleet which included both double- and single-deckers. The three Plaxton-bodied Leyland Panthers of 1971, of which this is one, passed to Hants & Dorset and the last was withdrawn last year.*

Right: *King Alfred was one of very few independents to buy the AEC/Park Royal Bridgemaster new. One of the pair delivered in 1961 is seen six years later.*

Left: *Another operator of double-deckers in the south was Seaview Services in the Isle of Wight which continued to use this 1950 all-Leyland Titan PD2 for more than 20 years. For some time it was the only Leyland psv on the island.*

Centre left: *The route between Three Bridges and Horsham suffered many vicissitudes over the years with Comfy Coaches, followed by the F. H. Kilner section of Hants & Sussex, London Transport and North Downs. None found much traffic offering. Here an ex-Western Welsh Harrington-bodied Albion Nimbus still in WW livery is seen on a North Downs journey leaving Crawley for Horsham.*

Below: *Other operations of which little trace remains were the old-established services of Dengate of Beckley. After some difficulties the business was taken over by Davie's of Rye but the stage services with eight buses were later transferred to Maidstone & District. One of the vehicles which was handed over was the Ford R192 with Willowbrook body which is seen at Dengate's Hastings terminus.*

Right: *The other operations of Davie's have endured and among the coaches has been this 1963 AEC Reliance which began with Glenton Tours and passed to Green Bus, Rugeley, which had it fitted with a 1968 Plaxton body. When Midland Red took over Green Bus it numbered it 2169 but did not operate it and it passed to Davie's.*

Bottom right; *The Folkestone-Hythe service of Sarjeant Bros, Folkestone, survived the war and was not taken over by East Kent until 1952. In this view in Red Lion Square, Hythe an Emcol-bodied Bedford WTB stands in front of an austerity-bodied Guy Arab of East Kent.*

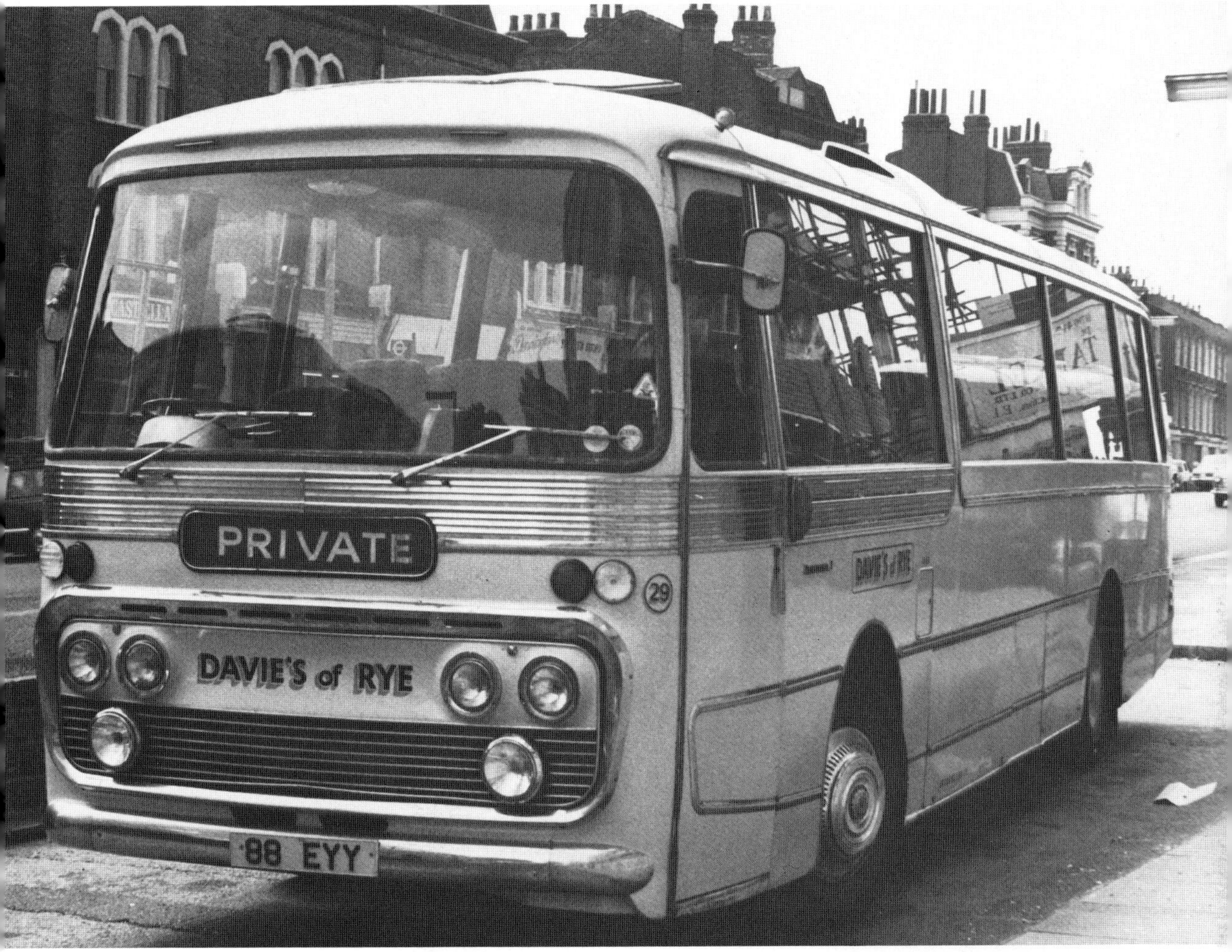
PRIVATE
DAVIE'S of RYE
88 EYY
29
DAVIE'S of RYE

EAST KENT

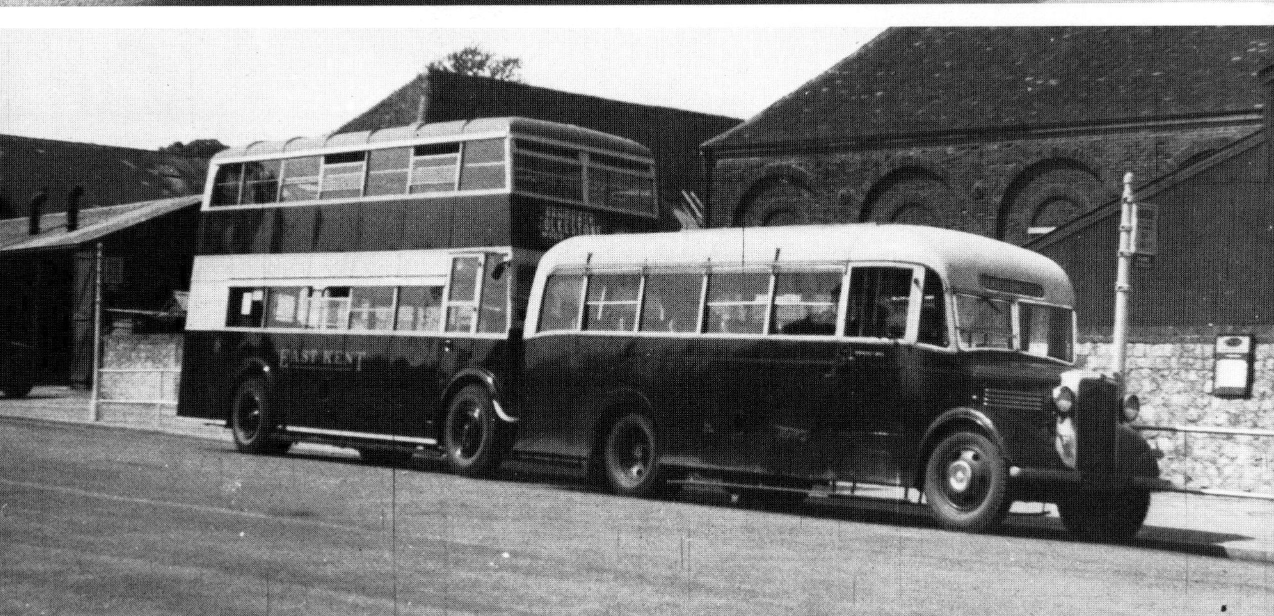

GNO-121

SARGENTS OF EAST GRINSTEAD
PRIVATE
GPM 450

Top left: *Bus operations of Ashline, Tonbridge developed to an extent in 1944 and were extended further in 1948 but, in the same year, the stage services passed to Maidstone & District. One of the vehicles used was this Dodge with Duple bodywork ex- Black & White, Leyton.*

Left: *Moving westwards there were the services of Sargents of East Grinstead in the Edenbridge-Crowborough-East Grinstead triangle. Maintained by Bedford OBs, the services passed to Maidstone & District by way of Southdown and London Transport. No 03 is seen in Edenbridge.*

Above: *Horsham is not the centre for independents that it was when this view was taken in Carfax with a Southdown Leyland Cub on a town service passing a Gilford 1660T of Comfy Coaches.*

Right: *In Horsham on the same afternoon was this Bedford WTB of Mitchell, Warnham (CLY 804).*

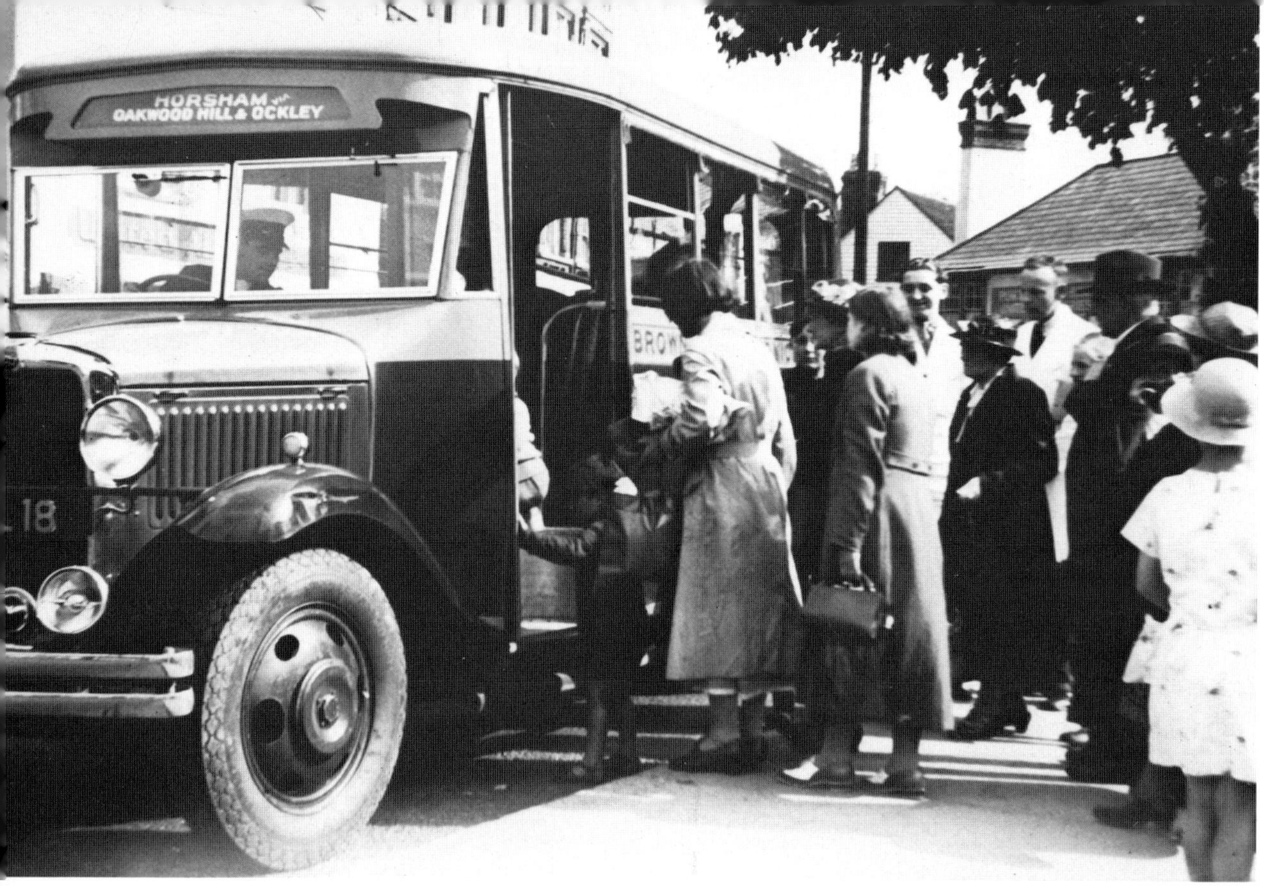
HORSHAM
OAKWOOD HILL & OCKLEY

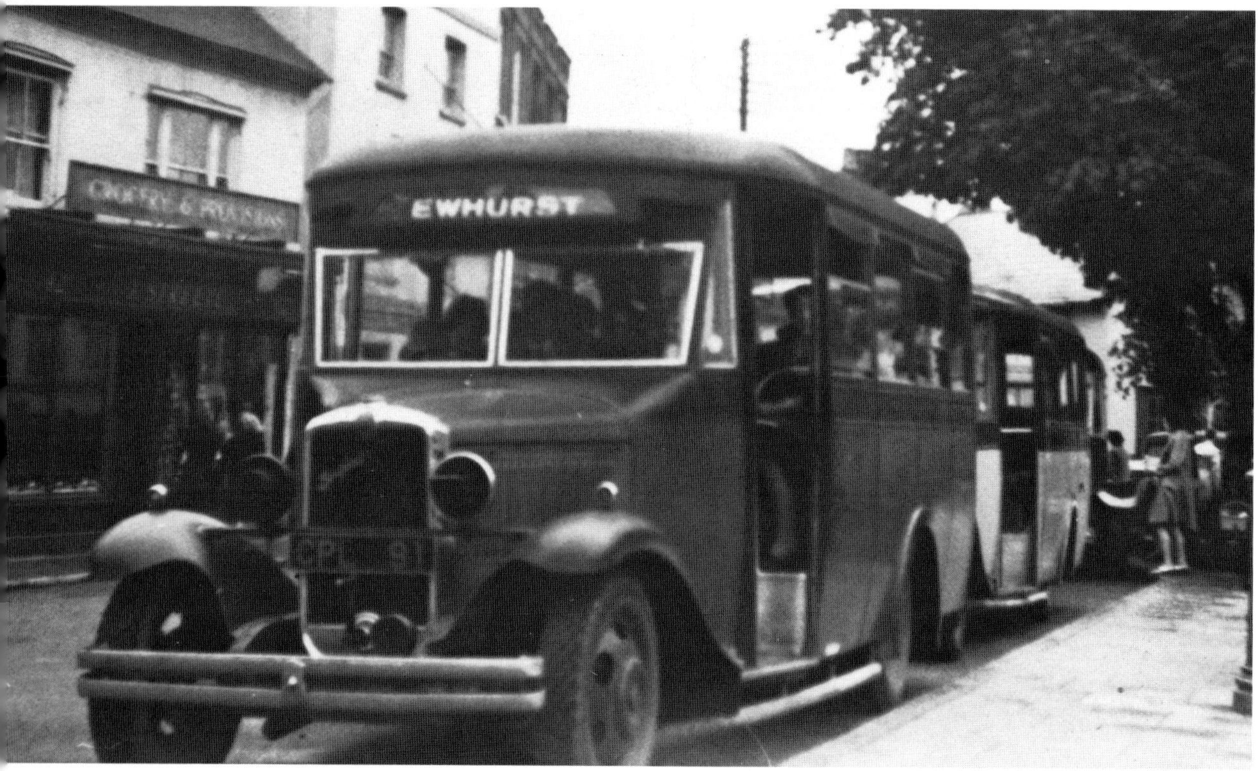
EWHURST

Top left: *A load waits to board a Bedford WLB of Brown Motor Service (Brady) in Horsham Carfax.*

Left: *By 1943 the same Bedford had passed to Ewhurst & District (Lazzell) — it went on later to Cream Line, Bordon.*

Above: *Nearly 30 years after the Mitchell Bedford picture was taken, that operator was in Horsham with this Leyland Tiger PS2 bodied by King & Taylor, Godalming.*

Right: *Tillingbourne Bus, which succeeded Tillingbourne Valley, replaced the Horsham-Rusper-Colgate-Horsham route on which the Mitchell Tiger was operating and an ex-Western National Bristol SUL is seen at Colgate.*

Above: *The Tillingbourne operations have extended in a variety of directions including, until August 1980, a route which reached Chichester on certain Wednesdays. This traversed part of the old Hants & Sussex territory. Southern Motorways (B. S. Williams Ltd) still maintains quite a sizeable part of the H&S operations and one of its Van Hool-bodied Fords is seen at Petersfield station on the service to Midhurst via Milland.*

Left: *Blue Saloon, of Guildford, evoking some nostalgia with its fleetname, has developed two local services which cover a number of roads otherwise unserved and some relinquished by Tillingbourne. Vehicles used have included ex-London Transport RFs, one of which is seen in Commercial Road bus station, Guildford.*

Top right: *Safeguard Coaches Ltd is probably the best known of the Guildford area independents these days. Apart from extended tours and seasonal express services it has a number of local services, several being worked in conjunction with Alder Valley. One of its bus-bodied Leyland Leopards leaves the bus station for Park Barn Estate via Woodbridge Hill in December 1979.*

Right: *Use of Railair link provided by Charles Rickards between Woking station and London Heathrow is considerable and this Leyland Leopard seen at Chertsey (Bell Corner) would seem to show this. Opening of the M25 motorway to Addlestone obviated the need to pass through Chertsey.*

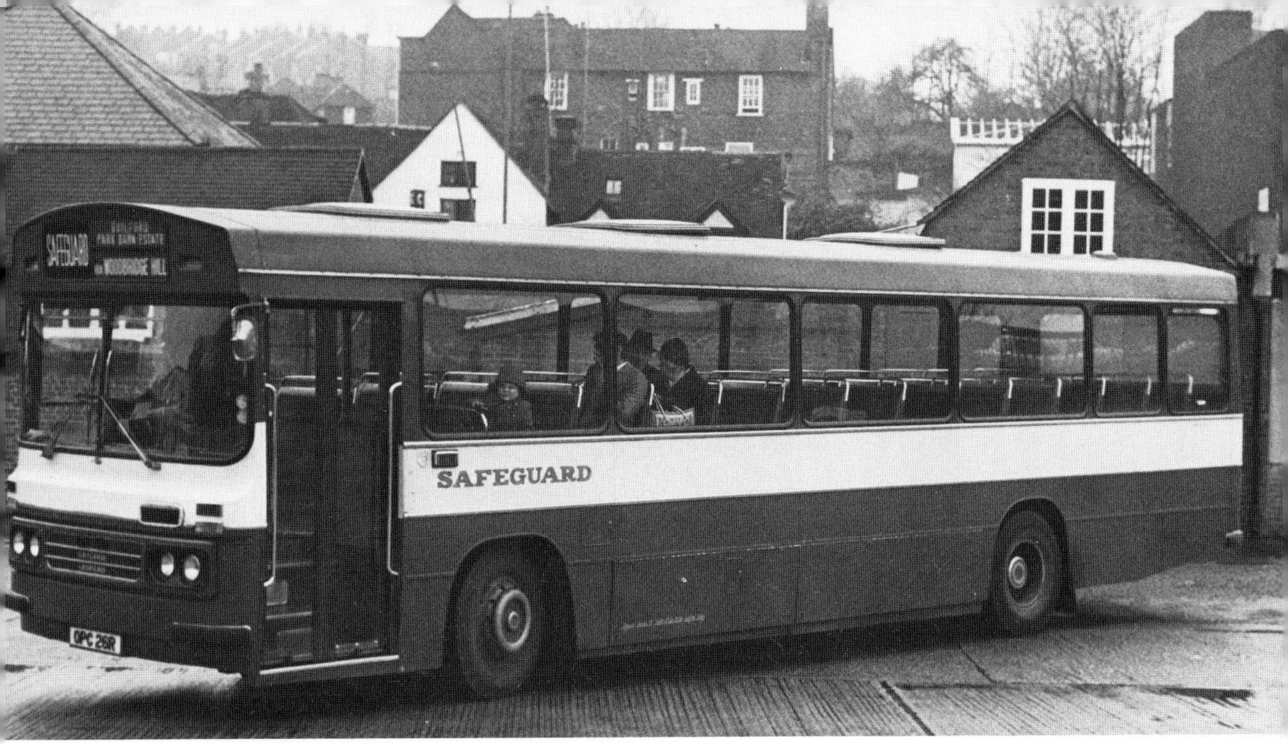

SAFEGUARD
SAFEGUARD

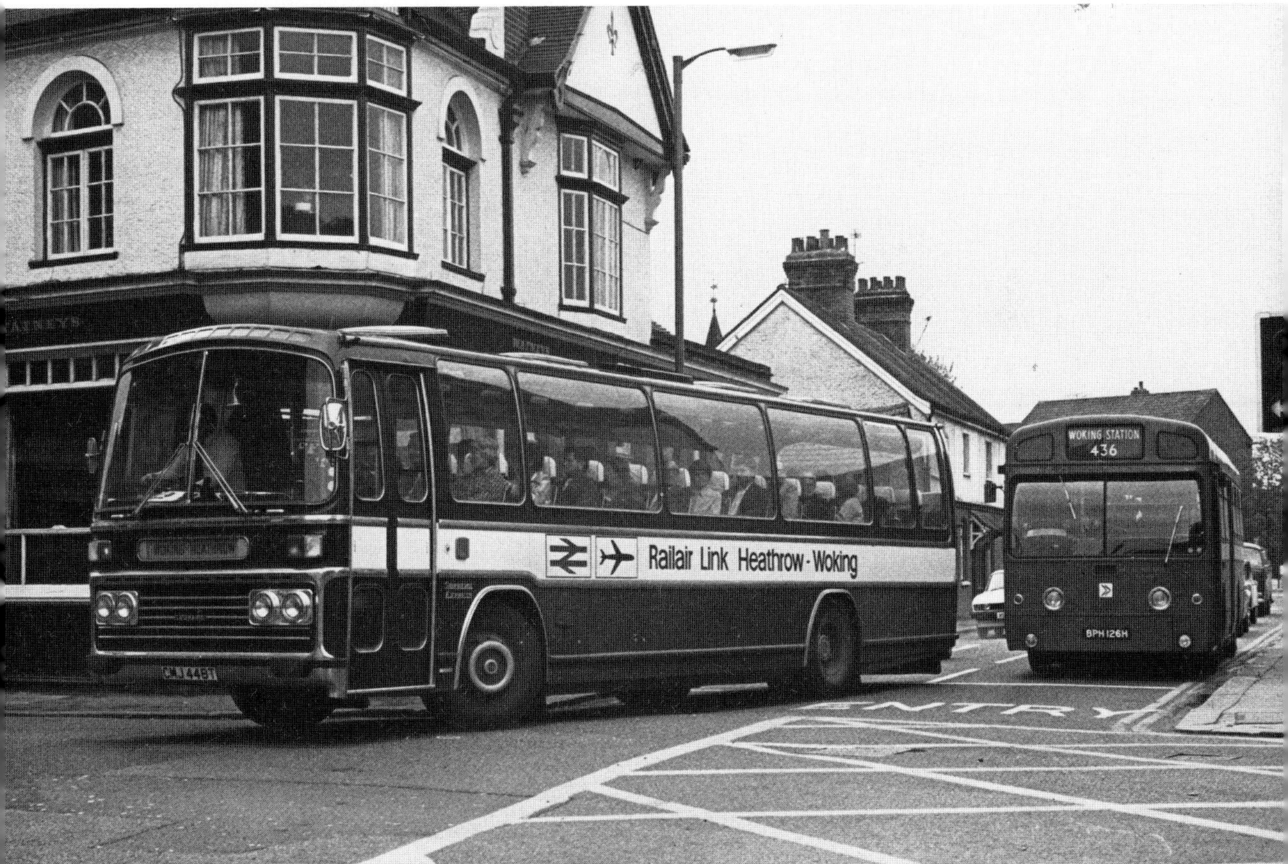

Railair Link Heathrow - Woking
WOKING STATION
436

Above: *With the passage of control of Smiths of Reading to the same concern as controls Windsorian Coaches there was a subsequent livery change and this former London Transport Marshall-bodied AEC Swift is in white with a blue band carrying vertical red stripes.*



Below: *For long a household name as Whites of Camberley with, at one time, a regular service to London, the firm has bases also at Hursley and at Baughurst. In 1978 it took delivery of its first double-decker, an ex-Nottingham City Transport Leyland Atlantean dating from 1965. It has a Metro-Cammell body.*

# East Anglian Independents

Although some of the substantial independent operators based in, or serving East Anglia have now gone, the area remains a stronghold of quite substantial businesses, some with double-deckers in their fleet. The City Coach Co Ltd, a company of particular interest by reason of its relationship to City, a major independent bus operator in London until formation of the London Passenger Transport Board in 1933, passed to Eastern National in 1952 which also took over Moore Bros (Kelvedon) Ltd. Smaller but nonetheless important were the associated Benfleet and District and Canvey & District which were bought by Westcliff early in 1951. The substantial Hicks Bros business based on Braintree was bought by the British Transport Commission in 1950 and handed over to the Eastern National to operate.

Wellknown names which have vanished recently have been Burwell & District and Suttons Coaches, of Clacton-on-Sea. An old-established operator S. Blackwell & Sons, Earls Colne, has passed to Hedingham & District Omnibuses and many others of varying antiquity abound such as H. C. Chambers & Son Ltd, Bures, W. Norfolk & Son, Nayland, Mulley's Motorways, Ixworth, Premier Travel Services, Cambridge, G. W. Osborne & Sons, Tollesbury, Whippet Coaches, Fenstanton, C. J. Partridge & Son, Hadleigh, Theobalds Coaches, Long Melford and Morley's Grey, West Row.

*Below: One of the East Anglian independents now departed was Burwell & District, a business which engendered much local loyalty in the area between Cambridge and Newmarket. Buses were bought both new and secondhand and exampels of the latter photographed in 1975 were two Weymann-bodied AEC Reliances. That on the left had come that year from Colchester Corporation after being new to Salford Corporation, while that on the right had come from Aldershot & District in 1973.*

B&D
BURWELL & DISTRICT
MOTOR SERVICE
50 NAU

DELAINE
DELAINE
ACT 540L

Left: *It could, however, be said that Burwell & District had a particular affection for Daimlers. This particular Fleetline was the second to come to B&D from the Nottingham City Transport fleet and was the first bus to carry the old style fleetname for over 20 years. Another unusual feature was the lower front end which had been grafted on to the square Park Royal original after an accident in 1970. The picture was taken in November 1976.*

Bottom left: *The Delaine, of Bourne, has a long-standing name for the smartness of its fleet and this is exemplified by the Northern Counties-bodied Leyland Atlantean seen entering Peterborough bus station in the spring of 1973.*

Right: *Leaving Huntingdon for Hilton in 1963 is a 1949 Leyland Titan PD2/3 of Whippet Coaches, Hilton. This Brush-bodied bus had come from Ribble three years earlier and remained with Whippet until the autumn of 1967.*

Below: *In later years Whippet has turned to rear-engined double-deckers, some of them secondhand including several Leyland Atlanteans from Greater Glasgow PTE. That illustrated was formerly Glasgow LA342.*

Above: *Premier Travel Services of Cambridge is well known partly because of the extensive network of express services which it has developed to many parts of Britain often in partnership with other operators. One partnership, albeit on a shorter service is that between Cambridge and Oxford which is shared with Percivals. A 1980 view at Gloucester Green, Oxford, shows a Percival Bedford and a Premier Travel AEC Reliance. The latter type of chassis was bought by PT until production ceased. Percivals has bases in both Oxford and Cambridge.*

Left: *In past years Premier Travel operated double-deckers to a quite considerable extent many of them being obtained secondhand from major operators. Exceptions were three Daimler CVD6s bought new in 1950 with Wilks & Meade bodies. They bore the names of counties and the last survivor of the trio was 'County of Cambridge' seen at the Chrishall depot in 1966.*

Bottom left: *More typical of the PT double-deckers were, however, the ex-Ribble Leyland Titans known as the White Ladies, one of which is seen also at Chrishall.*

Top right: *Withdrawn by London Transport in March 1968 this Leyland RTL passed to Colin S. Pegg of Caston and saw more than six years further service before it was withdrawn. It is seen in RAF Marham married quarters.*

Right: *A large-capacity single-deck in the Pegg fleet was this 1962 AEC Reliance with 65-seat Willowbrook body. It came from H & C, Garston in the spring of 1965.*

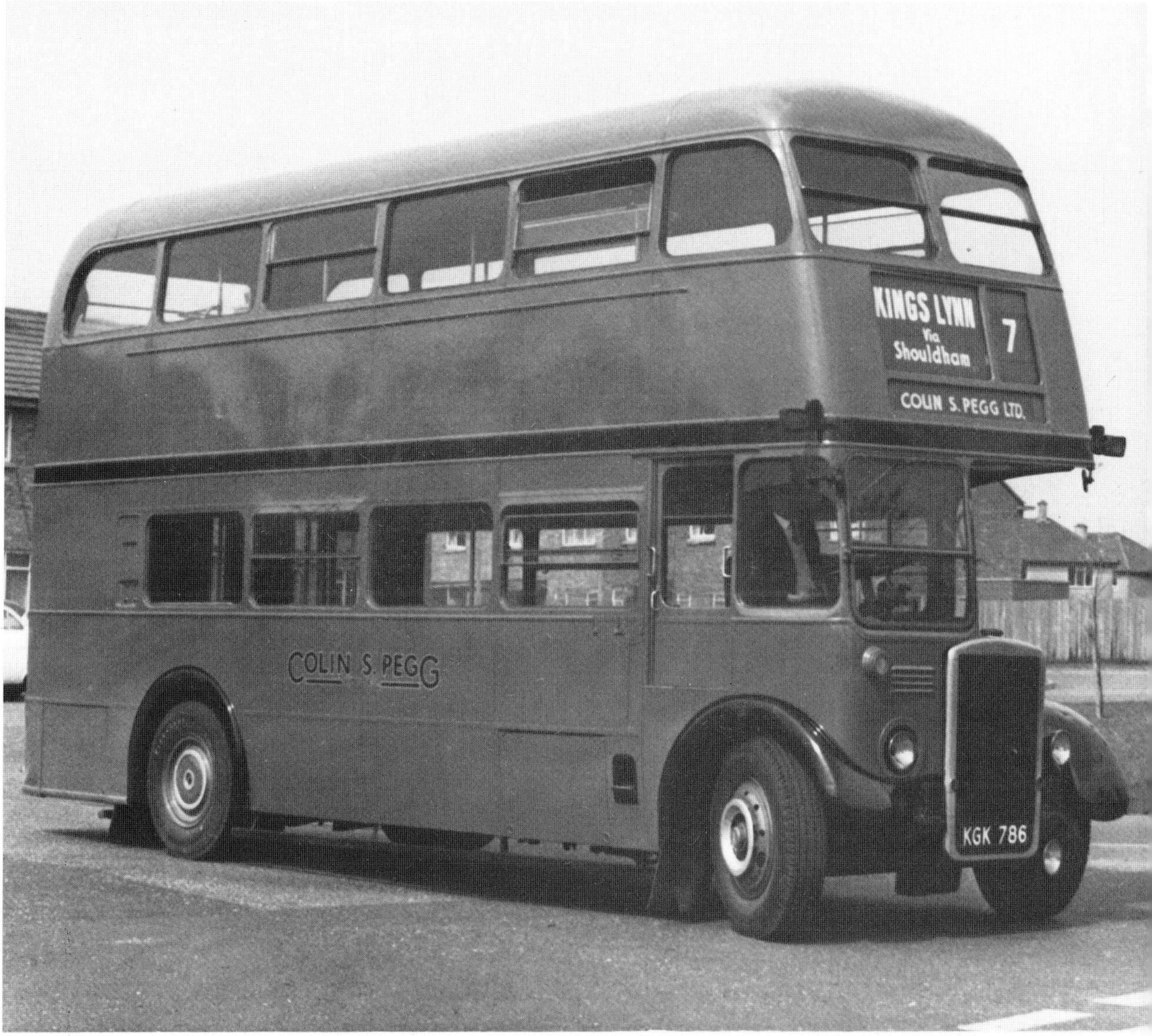
KINGS LYNN
Via
Shouldham
7
COLIN S. PEGG LTD.
COLIN S. PEGG
KGK 786

SWAFFHAM
858 GNM

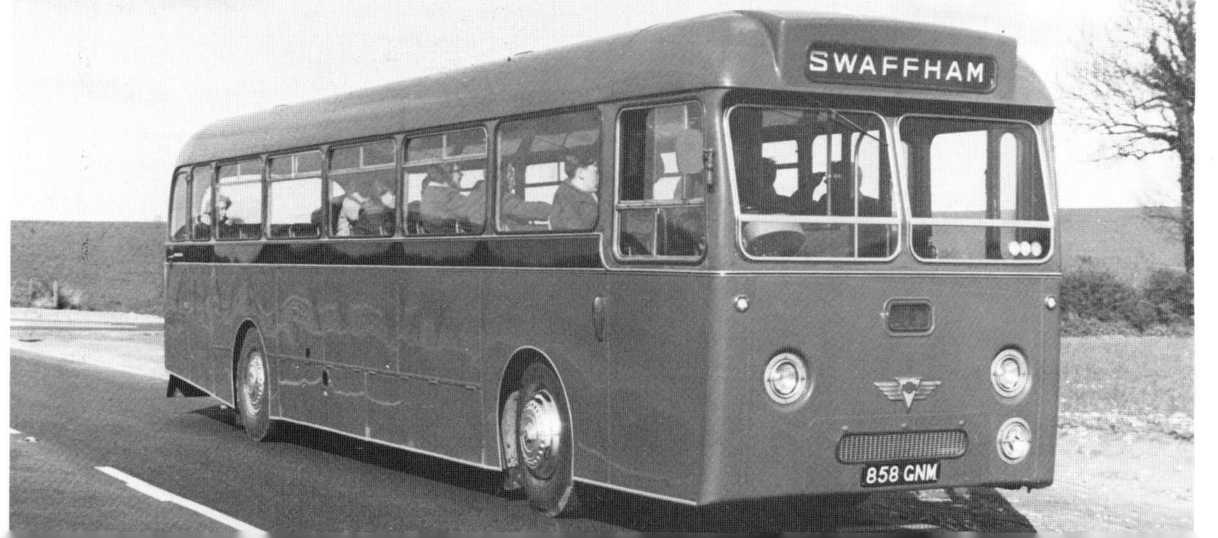

*Left: Seen regularly in Norwich after joining the fleet of R. O. Simonds, Diss was this Plaxton-bodied Ford.*

*Below: Also in the Norwich area is this Bristol KSW5G of Cullings which was previously with Eastern National.*

*Right: In the late 1950s A. C. Aldis operated his service between Felixstowe and Bawdsey Ferry with this Thurgood-bodied Guy Vixen previously with Our Bus, Grays.*

*Bottom right: Reference was made earlier to the cessation of bus operation by the Waveney District Council as heir to Lowestoft Corporation. An AEC Swift with Eastern Coach Works body passed to Bickers, of Coddenham.*

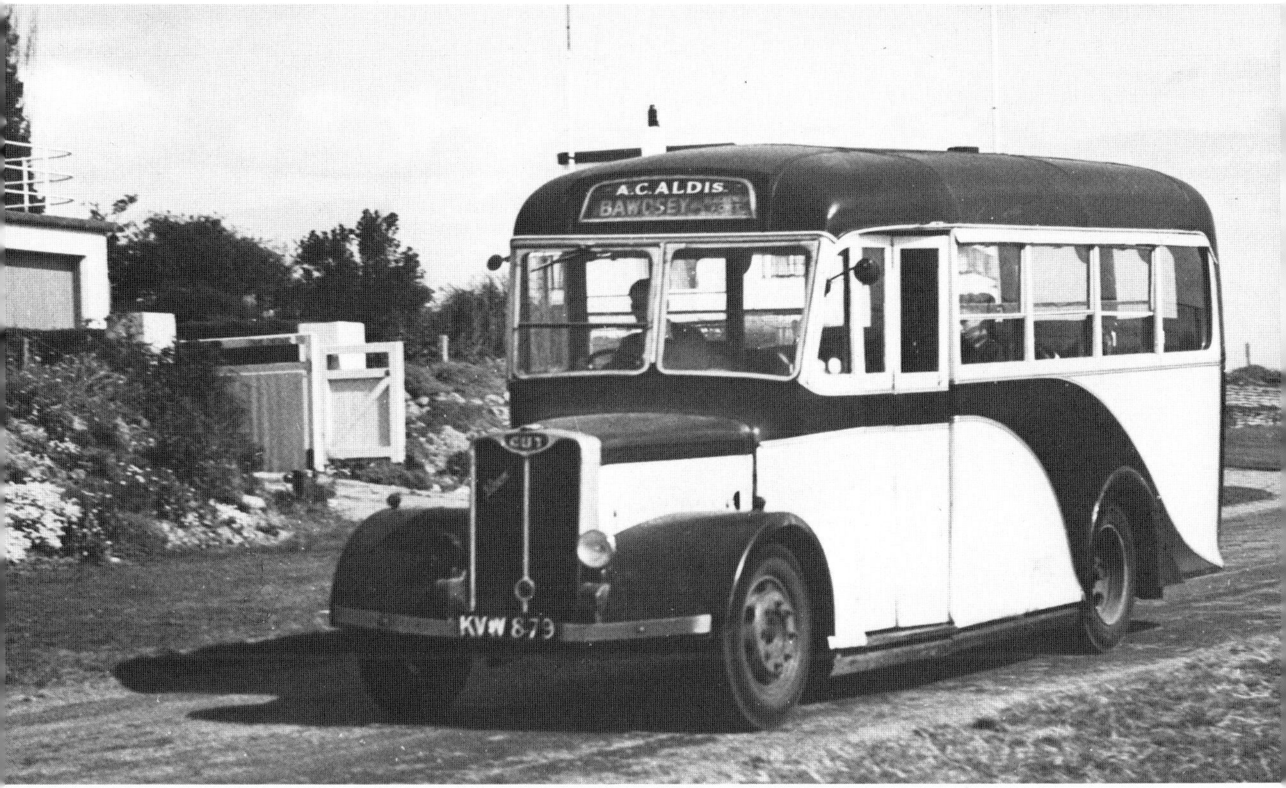
A.C.ALDIS
KVW 879

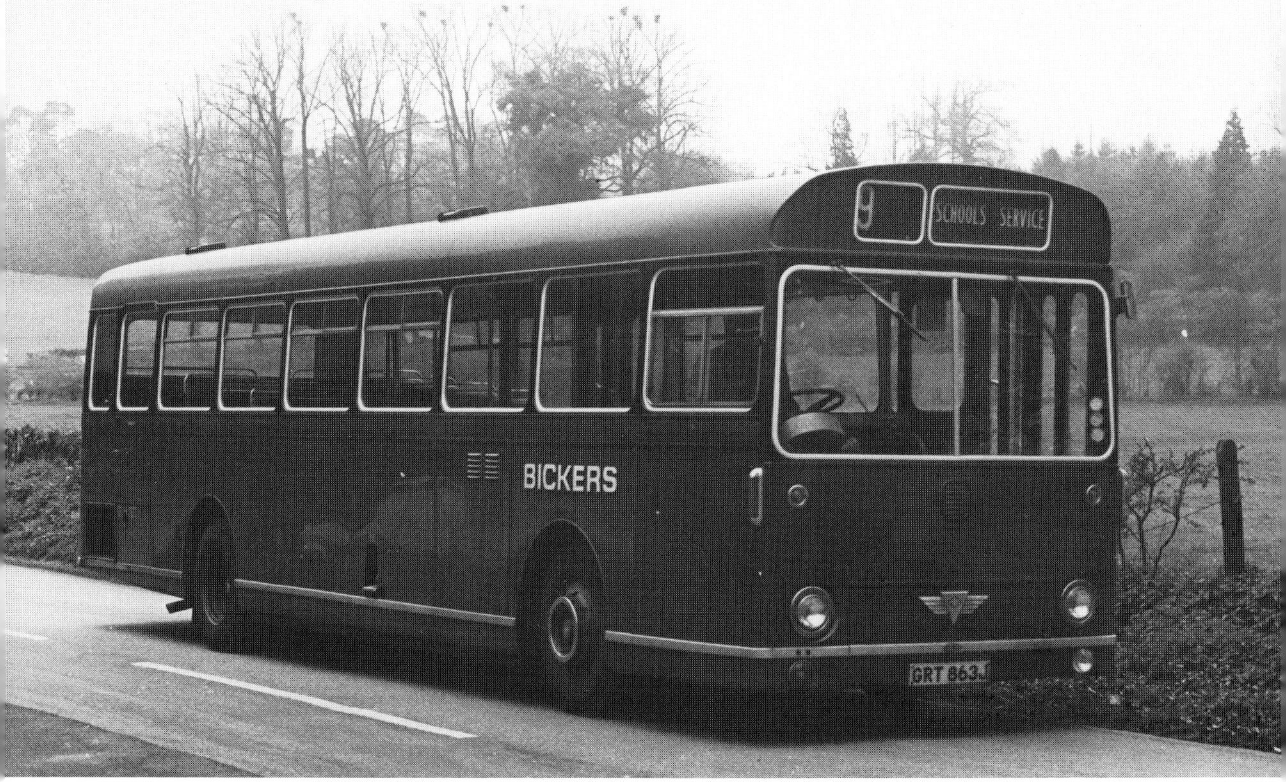
SCHOOLS SERVICE
BICKERS
GRT 863J

Above: *Still treating Suffolk operators, Rules of Boxford received in September 1960 a Yeates-bodied Bedford OB which had been operated by Stockdale, of Beccles.*

Below: *Some five years after its delivery this Plaxton-bodied AEC Reliance of P&M Coach Line, Ipswich was photographed in the Suffolk village of Brantham.*

Above: *An unusual coach operated by Goldsmiths of Sicklesmere was this 24-seat Austin 3K/CFED3 with Strachans bodywork which was new to the Shell plant at Ellesmere Port in 1955 and reached Goldsmiths by way of Wizard Fireworks of Chedburgh, Suffolk.*

Below: *Another vehicle which saw ordinary stage service later in its life was this Bedford SB5 of 1965, which also had Strachans bodywork and began its life with West Park Hospital, Epsom. It became a psv with C. J. Partridge & Son (H. A. C. Claireaux), Hadleigh.*

Left; *A Park Royal-bodied AEC Regent III of City of Oxford which joined the fleet of Theobolds, Long Melford in 1964 and saw six years service before its withdrawal. It is seen in Glemsford Broadway in 1966.*

Below: *Mulleys Motorways, of Ixworth, was at one time associated with the use of Gilford coaches and later tended to employ some of the less usual chassis or bodies. Leyland Comets were not all that common in Britain as passengers vehicles but this example with Duple body entered service in 1950 and operated for 20 years.*

Bottom left: *Another Mulley vehicle, which came from East Kent in August 1959 and was scrapped in December 1967, was this Guy Arab II with Weymann bodywork to austerity specifications.*

Top right: *When this ex-Nottingham Daimler Fleetline was photographed passing through Stoke-by-Nayland in June 1977 in the service of W. Norfolk & Son, Nayland, it was wearing the Queen's Silver Jubilee insignia.*

Right: *Two of the seven AEC Regal III coaches with Havington bodies which dated from 1949 and came from Maidstone & District. They were operated by Braybrooke of Mendlesham largely on American air base school contracts from 1961 to 1969.*

Norfolk's
COLCHESTER
64 RTO
BRAYBROOKE'S
PRIVATE 12
BRAYBROOKE'S
MELTON
SPECIAL
A.F.BRAYBROOKE & SON
KKK 833
KKK 839

Above: *A less usual type of coach which spent 5 years in the Norfolk fleet before it was withdrawn in 1968 was this 1952 AEC Regal IV with Whitson bodywork. It was new to Ripponden & District and passed subsequently to Hebble.*

Left: *Although its headquarters are in London, Grey-Green is closely associated with the provision of East Anglian services. One of its Plaxton-bodied Leyland Leopards is seen passing through Ipswich on its way from Great Yarmouth to London.*

Top right: *The first vehicle of Wicks, Braintree, in 1958 was this Commer Commando bodied by Harrington in 1946. It was operated by Black, of Delabole and passed to Southern National as its 3803 in 1952.*

Right: *Lodge, of High Eastern, bought this AEC Regent V. Willowbrook which was new to South Wales Transport in 1961. It is seen in Colchester bus station in the spring of 1972.*

PRIVATE    E.M.WICKS
FINE
DECORATION
WORLD
THE
AMAZING
CRITCH
HIS OWN STORY
B. BRIG GEN
MAC CRITCHLEY
JAF 586

LODGE COACHES
HIGH
EASTER
YCY 804

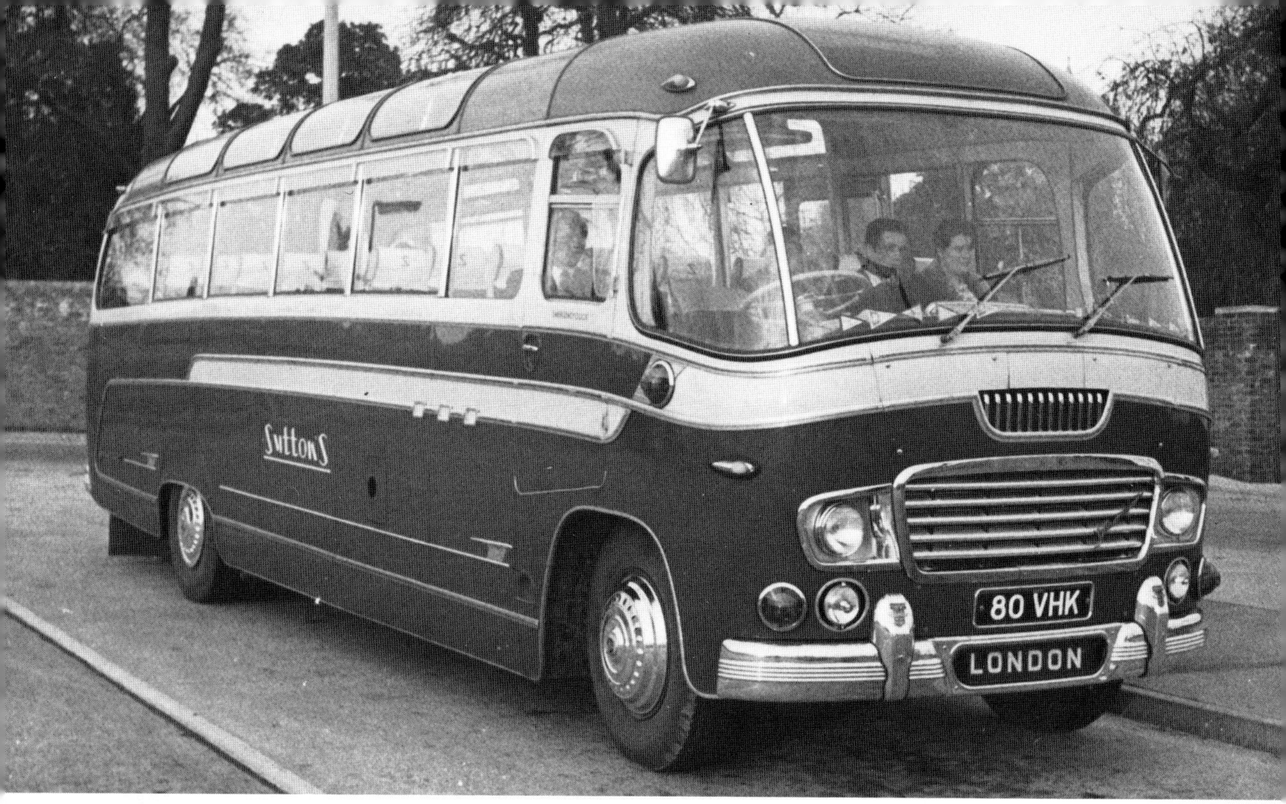
Suttons
80 VHK
LONDON

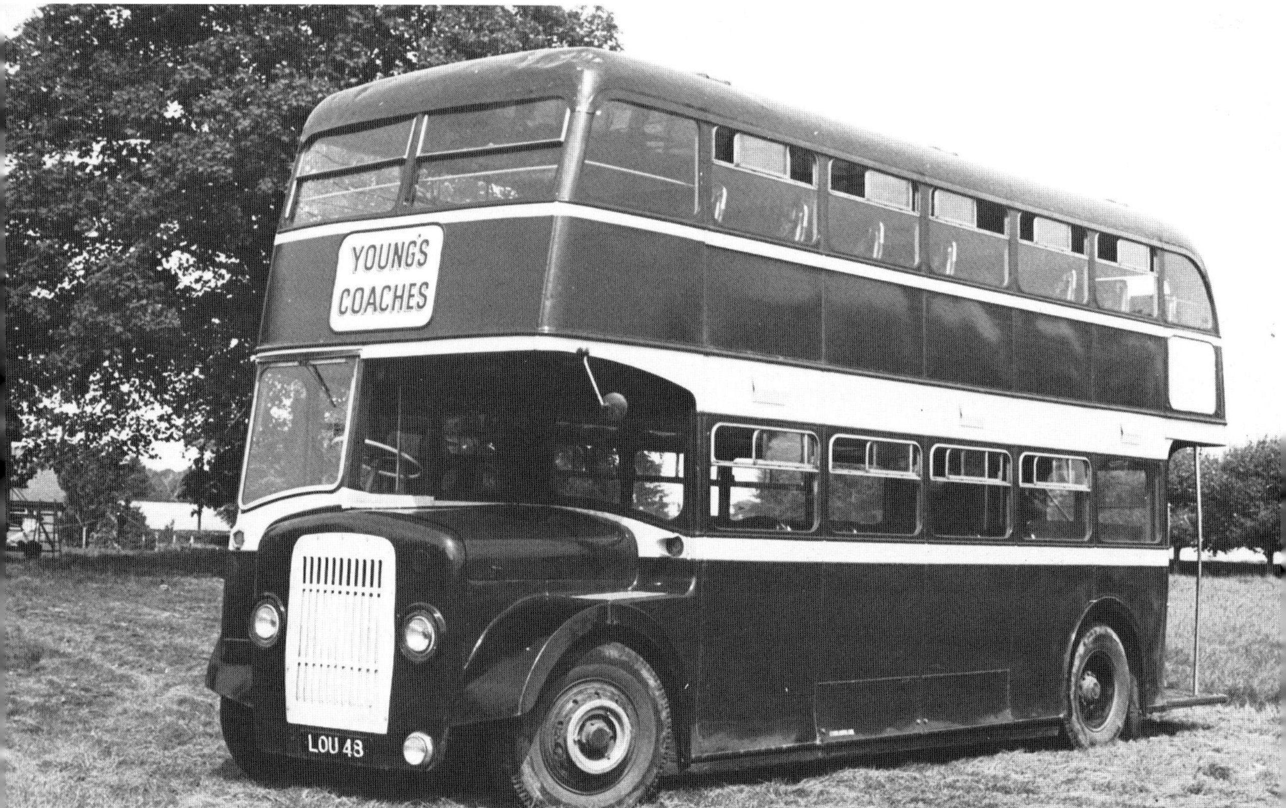
YOUNG'S
COACHES
LOU 48

Top left: *Suttons Coaches, Clacton-on-Sea, until 1978 operated a coach service to London. In 1961 it bought its first Ford, a 570E with Duple body, which it ran for 10 years. The coach is seen in Colchester in 1967.*

Left: *Another of the secondhand double-deckers which abounded in East Anglia at one time was this 1953 Dennis Lance with East Lancs body which Youngs of Rampton bought from Aldershot & District in 1965 and used for four years. It is seen at Lode.*

Above: *Blackwells of Earls Colne has latterly been controlled by Hedingham & District and has now been absorbed. In early 1960s it was operating this AEC Regal IV with Yeates bodywork which was new to Robin Hood, Nottingham in 1953.*

Below: *Hedingham & District bought the 1938 prototype Bristol L5G in 1962 and operated it for a year. Its body dated from 1950 and has been fitted to the chassis by the Bristol Omnibus Company in 1957. It is seen in Sible Hedingham.*

Left: *A 1980 addition to the Hedingham fleet is the ex-London Transport DMS seen at the Southend bus rally. Unlike many of the operators who have bought the discarded Fleetlines the two-door arrangement has been retained.*

Below: *Osbornes of Tollesbury, another of the old-established operators in East Anglia was operating this Plaxton-bodied Leyland Leopard in 1971. It came from Birch Bros and had previously carried Willowbrook bodywork.*

Right: *Still another old hand is H. C. Chambers & Son, Bures, which in 1969 took two Yeates-bodied Belfast SB5s from the Delaine fleet. They are seen on Angel Hill, Bury St Edmunds.*

Bottom right: *A more recent Chambers vehicle is this Plaxton-bodied Bedford YRT seen climbing out of Bures en route to Colchester in April 1977.*

CHAMBERS
CHAMBERS
UTL 78
ACT 101B

COLCHESTER
CHAMBERS
LDX 840P

Above: *A unique double-decker was this Alexander-bodied Leyland Titan PD 3/2 with Homalloy front which figured in the 1957 Scottish show. After trials with both Western SMT and Central SMT it went into service with Highland from which it passed in December 1976 to Avro, of Corringham.*

Below: *Well known in South Essex, Harris Coaches of Grays was for long a user of Leyland Leopards but has turned in recent years to Volvos and later DAFs. One of the Volvos with Plaxton bodywork is seen here in Basildon.*